AIR CAMPAIGN

SCHWEINFURT–REGENSBURG 1943

Eighth Air Force's costly early daylight battles

MARSHALL L. MICHEL III   ILLUSTRATED BY JIM LAURIER

OSPREY PUBLISHING
Bloomsbury Publishing Plc

Kemp House, Chawley Park, Cumnor Hill, Oxford OX2 9PH, UK
29 Earlsfort Terrace, Dublin 2, Ireland
1385 Broadway, 5th Floor, New York, NY 10018, USA
Email: info@ospreypublishing.com
www.ospreypublishing.com

OSPREY is a trademark of Osprey Publishing Ltd

First published in Great Britain in 2020
Transferred to digital print in 2024

A catalog record for this book is available from the British Library.

Print ISBN: 978 1 4728 3867 4
ePub: 978 1 4728 3868 1
ePDF: 978 1 4728 3865 0
XML: 978 1 4728 3866 7

Maps by www.bounford.com
3D BEVs by Paul Kime
Diagrams by Adam Tooby
Index by Alan Rutter
Typeset by PDQ Digital Media Solutions, Bungay, UK
Printed and bound in India by Replika Press Private Ltd.

24 25 26 27 28   10 9 8 7 6 5 4 3 2

The Woodland Trust
Osprey Publishing supports the Woodland Trust, the UK's leading woodland
conservation charity.

www.ospreypublishing.com
To find out more about our authors and books visit our website. Here you
will find extracts, author interviews, details of forthcoming events and the
option to sign-up for our newsletter.

CONTENTS

INTRODUCTION

A classic picture of the most numerous and important VIII Bomber Command bomber, the B-17F. The B-17 was valued for its toughness and because it was easy to fly in the tight formations necessary for mutual protection, though British bombers carried a much heavier bomb load. (National Archives and Records Administration – NARA)

When the United States of America entered World War II its most useful ally was the United Kingdom, which had already been at war for more than two years, and the two quickly acted to coordinate their war objectives. At the Arcadia Conference in Washington from December 22, 1941 to January 14, 1942, the British and Americans agreed that Germany was the most dangerous enemy and its defeat was the first priority, which would mean an invasion of Europe. But first the Luftwaffe and Germany's industrial capabilities had to be reduced, and to that end America began to build a bomber and fighter force, designated the Eighth Air Force and based in the United Kingdom, which would initially be responsible for the American air offensive against Germany. Most of the American air leaders were products of the Air Corps Tactical School, and this school gave American airmen their prewar air doctrine, that unescorted but heavily armed bombers attacking critical targets with daylight precision bombing were the key to victory in war. Eighth Air Force Bomber Command (VIII Bomber Command) would be committed to this doctrine for most of 1943.

With the Germans seemingly likely to conquer Russia, almost in desperation in April 1942 the American military proposed that the Allies invade Europe in mid-1943 in Operation *Roundup*, and even offered a minor invasion, Operation *Sledgehammer*, in late 1942 if necessary. The British demurred, and in July 1942 US President Roosevelt discarded this idea and instead ordered the American armed forces to support the invasion of North Africa, Operation *Torch*, in November 1942. This would allow American forces to engage the Germans in land combat (the British were already fighting in the Western Desert) and the invasion of Europe would be left until it was assured of success.

Eighth Air Force had been building slowly since 1942, but to support *Torch* the command was gutted, stripped of the bulk of its B-24s, many of its B-17s, and virtually all of its P-38 fighters. This diversion of resources to *Torch* significantly delayed the Eighth's development of a combat capability. Major General Ira C. Eaker was named commander of the Eighth Air Force on December 1, 1942.

When Roosevelt, Churchill, and other allied leaders met at the Casablanca Conference in January 1943, one of the things they agreed to do was to attack Germany with bombers until a land invasion was possible. The Royal Air Force (RAF) Bomber Command argued for the RAF's plan for night area bombing of German cities, but American Generals George C. Marshall (US Army Chief of Staff), Henry "Hap" Arnold (Army Air Force Chief of Staff), and Eaker vigorously promoted the American plan for daylight precision strategic bombing. Eaker presented a briefing to Churchill, "The Case for Day Bombing," which he defined as round-the-clock bombing of Germany. Churchill liked this and accepted the idea.

There was important subtext to this. All of the Army Air Force leadership wanted their command to become independent of the army after the war, and they saw the daylight bombing campaign as a way to a postwar independent Air Force.

On May 18, 1943, the Combined Chiefs of Staff (CCS) approved the formal "Plan for the Combined Bomber Offensive from the United Kingdom," and in June 1943 the Combined Bomber Offensive (CBO) officially began. VIII Bomber Command was to begin its role in the CBO under the name of Operation *Pointblank*, but the CCS had made it clear to the US Army Air Force (USAAF) and the Eighth Air Force leadership that *Pointblank*'s objective was the defeat or destruction of the German day fighter force. *Pointblank* was only expected to prepare for an invasion, not to "win the war." While the RAF was included in *Pointblank*, at this point it simply could not hit German aircraft factories or airfields with any accuracy, so the destruction of the German day fighter force would be the responsibility of Eighth Air Force, as would most of the other targets that required precision bombing – the remainder of the German aircraft industry, ball bearing plants and oil.

On the German side, the Luftwaffe priorities at the beginning of 1943 were mainly offensive – the Eastern Front and the Mediterranean Front. Defensively, it was focused on RAF night bombing, and USAAF daylight bombing was its fourth concern. The day fighter organization, the Reichs-Luftverteidigung (Air Defense of the Reich or RLV), did have a robust day fighter defense on the English Channel/North Sea coast, with one elite *Jagdgeschwader* (fighter wing) comprising four groups, but there were virtually no fighter defenses in the center of the Reich.

Indeed, the Germans had generally neglected their daylight air defenses in the center of the country. The penetration of the tough American bombers was a new challenge to the Luftwaffe fighter pilots, but they began to develop new tactics in late 1942, when Adolf Galland (the chief of the German fighter force) and Erhard Milch (Air Inspector General) started to bring in fighters from Russia and the Mediterranean to bolster the Reich's defenses.

CHRONOLOGY

1941

December 22, 1941–January 14, 1942 At the Arcadia Conference in Washington the Allies agree to a "defeat Germany first" war plan.

1942

February 20 Army Air Forces chief Henry "Hap" Arnold orders the all-out development of external fuel tanks for American fighters.

April American military proposes that the Allies invade Europe in mid-1943, in Operation *Roundup*, or that they mount a smaller invasion, Operation *Sledgehammer*, in late 1942 if necessary. The British reject the idea.

April Eighth Air Force begins its buildup.

June First P-38s arrive in England.

July Roosevelt agrees with the British regarding operations *Roundup* and *Sledgehammer*, and orders the United States to support the invasion of North Africa, Operation *Torch*.

August 29 P-38s fly their first mission.

October–November Eighth Air Force is stripped of the bulk of its B-24s, many of its B-17s, and virtually all of its P-38 fighters to support *Torch*.

November 23 Hauptmann Egon Mayer leads the first Luftwaffe head-on attack on a formation of 36 B-17s attacking St Nazaire, shooting down four and seriously damaging another.

December 3 Sixty-eight bombers of VIII Bomber Command strike the St Nazaire U-boat base, the heaviest attack against submarine bases to date. Considerable damage is done to the dock area.

December 14 One squadron of 4th Fighter Group becomes the first in the United Kingdom to be completely equipped with P-47s.

December 27 Fifty-three heavy bombers make the first attack on Germany, bombing the naval base, U-boat construction works, power plant, and docks at Wilhelmshaven. Other heavy bombers bomb the submarine base at Emden.

1943

January At the Casablanca Conference, the Allies agree to attack Germany with bombers. General Ira Eaker, Eighth Air Force commander, presents a briefing to Churchill, "The Case for Day Bombing," meaning round-the-clock bombing. Churchill accepts the idea. The CCS issue the "Casablanca Directive," which broadly outlines the operations of the bomber forces of the United States and Britain located in the United Kingdom. Primary targets listed in order of priority are submarine construction yards, the Luftwaffe and aircraft industry, transportation, oil plants, and other war industries.

January VIII Bomber Command begins to experiment with formation bombing.

February 24 General Eaker, commander of Eighth Air Force, is advised by the War Department of the CCS of the decision to employ his fighter units primarily in an offensive role in support of bombers.

February Three P-47 groups are fully equipped in the United Kingdom but not combat ready due to engine and serious radio problems.

March 4 Forty-two heavy bombers fly missions over Germany and the Netherlands, hitting the shipyards at Rotterdam and attacking the Hamm rail yards. This is the first attack on a Ruhr industrial target.

March 10 P-47s take part for the first time in a fighter sweep from the United Kingdom. Aircraft-to-aircraft communication proves impossible because of VHF radio malfunctions.

March 18 Ninety-seven heavy bombers strike submarine yards at Vegesack. This mission marks the first successful combat use of automatic flight-control equipment (AFCE) linked with bombsights.

April 8 Two more P-47 groups, the 56th and 78th, become operational. Added to the already operational 4th Group, this enables VIII Fighter Command to prepare for its role of escorting bombers on deep penetrations into enemy territory.

April 26 115 B-17s bomb the Focke-Wulf factory at Bremen.

May 4 Sixty-five heavy bombers strike the former Ford and General Motors plants at Antwerp, with P-47s beginning to providing fighter escort out to 175 miles.

May 13 Avions Potez aircraft factory at Meaulte is attacked by 119 heavy bombers. Four additional B-17 groups become available for VIII Bomber Command combat operations.

May 14 A maximum effort marks the first time that more than 200 US bombers are dispatched from VIII Bomber Command. They attack four targets in Germany, the principal attack being against submarine yards and naval installations at Kiel.

May 18 The CCS approve the "Plan for the Combined Bomber Offensive (CBO) from the United Kingdom." VIII Bomber Command now has formal authorization to proceed with daylight strategic bombing. The CBO plan lists the destruction of German day fighter force as the priority objective.

May 21 VIII Bomber Command sends 123 bombers to hit German U-boat yards. The main effort is directed at Wilhelmshaven, while a smaller number of planes strike at Emden. At Wilhelmshaven, German fighters are reported as firing rockets for the first time.

May 29 A total of 147 heavy bombers hit submarine pens and locks at St Nazaire. Seven YB-40s, B-17s converted to heavily armored aircraft with great firepower to solve the problem of long-range escort for bombers, fly their first mission. The YB-40s are unable to keep up with the B-17s and show the need for modification of waist and tail-gun feeds and ammunition supplies.

June The Assistant Secretary of War for Air visits VIII Fighter Command and discusses the problems of fighter escort for the bombers.

June 7 VIII Bomber Command continues to send reinforcements to North Africa as a B-24 group originally scheduled for the United Kingdom is diverted to the Mediterranean.

June 10 The CCS issue the directive marking the official beginning of the CBO of the USAAF and RAF against sources of German war power. The RAF is to bomb strategic city areas at night, and the American force to hit precise targets by daylight. The CCS designate the

Combined Operational Planning Committee as the agency for coordinating the efforts of the CBO forces.

June 13 A total of 102 heavy bombers bomb the Bremen U-boat yards while a smaller force strikes at Kiel submarine yards and supporting infrastructure. The heaviest German fighter attack to date against Eighth Air Force accounts for 26 heavy bombers, most from the Kiel force.

June 15 Additional modifications of YB-40 escort bombers are completed.

June 22 In the first large-scale daylight raid on the Ruhr, 182 heavy bombers hit the Hüls chemical works and synthetic rubber plant. The plant is severely damaged. Eleven YB-40s accompany the Hüls raid; one is lost to flak.

June 25 A total of 167 heavy bombers attack Hamburg, but the targets are obscured by clouds. Of seven YB-40 escort bombers dispatched, only four are able to accompany formations to the target area.

June 26 Another B-24 group leaves the United Kingdom for North African duty as demands for the invasion of Sicily and a raid on the oil fields at Ploesti in Romania make further inroads on the strength of VIII Bomber Command. Thirty-nine heavy bombers hit the aircraft industry at Villacoublay near Paris, while five YB-40 escort bombers take off to accompany the heavy bombers but are all unable to complete the attack.

June 26 Arnold sends a cable to Eaker expressing concern about his employment of fighters, saying that too many are being used for fighter sweeps and not enough for bomber escort.

June 27 Another B-24 group leaves for North Africa as Eighth Air Force continues to send combat units to the Mediterranean.

July 1 General Frederick L. Anderson Jr replaces General Newton Longfellow as Commanding General VIII Bomber Command. The (British) Joint Intelligence Committee report maintains that the CBO has caused Germany to adopt a defensive air strategy, resulting in more than half its fighter strength being employed on the Western Front at the expense of the Eastern and Mediterranean fronts, as well as causing considerable damage to transportation, the synthetic rubber industry, and the fuel, iron, and coal industries of the Ruhr.

July VIII Bomber Command officially begins formation bombing for all units. Each B-17 bombardment wing is given a white symbol containing a blue letter on the tail fin for group identification.

July 24 VIII Bomber Command executes a very successful attack on the nitrate works at Heroya. This is Eighth Air Force's first mission to Norway and its longest (a 1,900-mile round trip) to date. The crews successfully use a new assembly procedure for bad weather, whereby aircraft take off individually on instruments and proceed to a designated "splasher beacon" for group formation and then along a line of three more such beacons for force assembly. The method works well and makes possible many future missions which might otherwise have been abandoned.

July 25–30 Fortress Blitz week begins – seven targets in seven days planned to weaken German fighter defenses.

July 25 Following a raid the previous night during which RAF heavy bombers did tremendous damage, 218 heavy bombers bomb the shipyard at Hamburg and U-boat base at Kiel. Nineteen heavy bombers are lost, mostly to effective formation attacks by German fighters.

July 28 More than 300 heavy bombers are dispatched in two forces to bomb German targets. Bad weather prevents the majority from completing the mission, but 49 bomb aircraft works at Kassel and 28 attack the major Fw 190 factory at Oschersleben, making it the deepest US bomber penetration into Germany to date. However, 22 heavy bombers are lost as German fighters score their first effective results with rockets. One-hundred-and-five P-47s equipped with external belly tanks for the first time escort the B-17s into Germany, while other P-47s, going more than 30 miles deeper into Germany than they have penetrated before, meet the returning bombers. They surprise about 60 German fighters and destroy nine of them; one P-47 is lost.

July 30 One hundred and eighty-six B-17s attack the Kassel Fw 190 factories, and in the largest air battle to date P-47s with drop tanks shoot down 27 German fighters for the loss of seven P-47s and 17 B-17s.

August 17 On the first anniversary of US heavy bomber operations from England, 315 B-17s launch a two-pronged attack into Germany, targeting Schweinfurt and Regensburg, with the Regensburg strike force continuing to land in North Africa. The weather disrupts the timing of the operation and a total of 60 B-17s are lost.

The greatest – but not the deadliest – impediment to the American bombing campaign was the weather. Finally, in the fall of 1943, Eighth Air Force asked the RAF for some of its blind-bombing equipment. After testing several types of equipment, the Eighth settled on the *H2S* blind-bombing radar carried in a B-17 in the nose under a plastic blister. Soon there was an American version, the *H2X*, but both proved unreliable for much of 1943. (NARA)

August The chief of the German fighter force, Adolf Galland, tells Hitler and Göring that American fighters were shot down over Germany. They don't believe him.

September 6 Eighth Air Force sets a new record for the number of heavy bombers dispatched when 407 are sent to bomb aircraft and bearing factories in and around Stuttgart. Bad weather frustrates the bombing of the Stuttgart targets, strong fighter opposition is encountered, and 45 heavy bombers are lost.

September 8 Three B-24 groups return to the United Kingdom from Africa and resume operations.

September 9 A total of 330 US heavy bombers are dispatched to bomb airfields as well as industrial areas around Paris in Operation *Starkey*, designed to contain enemy forces in the west to prevent their transfer to the Eastern Front, and to serve as a dress rehearsal in the Pas de Calais area for the invasion of France. The Allies hope to provoke the Luftwaffe into a large air battle, but only a few Luftwaffe fighters engaged the heavily escorted bomber force.

September 13 VIII Bomber Command reorganizes. The 1st (B-17), 2nd (B-24), and 3rd (B-17) Bomb Divisions are activated in the United Kingdom, with each bomb division organized into combat bomb wings.

September 15 B-17s fly a night mission with the RAF against the Montlucon Dunlop tire factory.

September 16 B-17s fly a night mission with 340 RAF heavy bombers at the request of General Eisenhower. Three B-24 groups in the United Kingdom are sent back to North Africa for a second time at General Eisenhower's request for support in this theater.

September 23 B-17s join the RAF on a night raid to Mannheim.

September 27 Two B-17s equipped with *H2S* lead an attack of 244 other B-17s on the first large daylight mission against a cloud-covered target on the port area at Emden. P-47s with belly tanks escort the bombers the entire way to the target in Germany for the first time.

October 1 A report by the Eighth Air Force intelligence section shows that despite the recent efforts of the Allies to destroy the German aircraft industry, fighter production has expanded greatly and enemy fighter strength on the Western Front has increased.

October 2 About 340 heavy bombers led by two Pathfinders attack industrial areas of Emden.

October 4 A force of 282 heavy bombers attacks industrial areas of Frankfurt-am-Main, Wiesbaden, and the Saar; German defenses react poorly.

October 7–8 Göring holds a conference with his day fighter commanders to berate them about their performance.

October 8 More than 350 heavy bombers attack the city and industrial areas of Bremen and U-boat yards at Vegesack. For the first time Eighth Air Force uses airborne transmitters, *Carpet*, to jam German radar, but 30 US bombers are lost in the main attack on Bremen.

October 9–13 VIII Bomber Command begins five days of major strikes deep into Germany.

October 9 VIII Bomber Command launches a mass unescorted strike of B-17s and B-24s against targets in eastern Germany and Poland. The bombers were not intercepted until they were on their way back, but then the force lost 31 bombers.

October 10 VIII Bomber Command sent 236 bombers to Munster with escort the whole way, but the force lost 33 B-17s, though the P-47s shot down ten twin-engine rocket fighters.

October 14 Almost 230 heavy bombers attack the city area and ball bearing plants at Schweinfurt. Fierce opposition of great numbers of fighters, many of them firing rockets, accounts for 60 US aircraft shot down. As a result of these heavy losses, unescorted daylight bombing against strategic targets deep in Germany is suspended.

October 15 P-38s, just returned from North Africa, fly their first orientation mission.

October 16 The American Joint Chiefs of Staff send General Eisenhower a proposed directive, submitted by General Arnold on 9 October, for establishment of a new air force (Fifteenth) in Italy to be used when needed as part of a CBO against strategic targets in Germany.

October 29 USAAF commander General Arnold orders that all P-38 and P-51 production for the next three months is to be withheld from all other theaters and sent to the Eighth Air Force.

November 3 A total of 539 B-17s and B-24s, including 11 Pathfinders, nine using the RAF's *H2S* blind-bombing device and two using the American *H2X*, attack the port of Wilhelmshaven. This is the first blind-bombing mission in which the target is completely destroyed and is also the Eighth Air Force's first 500-plane mission. P-38s escort the heavy bombers almost the entire trip and see their first real combat, claiming three aircraft shot down.

November 5 A force of 436 heavy bombers, including nine Pathfinder aircraft, attacks oil plants at Gelsenkirchen and rail yards at Munster.

November 19 A total of 130 heavy bombers attack Gelsenkirchen, but malfunctioning of blind-bombing equipment results in no attacks on the primary target.

November 28–30 The Tehran Conference takes place; Roosevelt, Churchill, and Stalin discuss further action against Germany.

November 29 Over 250 heavy bombers attack the port of Bremen, but cloud conditions and malfunctioning of blind-bombing equipment cause most to abort; 13 aircraft are lost on the mission.

November 30 Seventy-eight heavy bombers hit industries at Solingen using blind-bombing equipment, but over 200 aircraft abort due to cloud formations which cause assembly difficulties and require flying at altitudes not feasible for the B-24s included in the mission.

December At the Sextant Conference, USAAF commander General Arnold announces that the American buildup in England has fallen well behind the rate that reinforcement planners had stated was necessary to achieve *Pointblank* objectives. A note from Air Chief Marshal Portal to CCS states that *Pointblank* is three months behind in relationship to the tentative date for *Overlord*, which has been set for May 1, 1944. This brings more pressure on Eighth Air Force to destroy the Luftwaffe fighter force and aircraft production plants.

December 1 A total of 281 heavy bombers hit industrial targets at Solingen after malfunctioning of Pathfinder equipment prevents an attack on the primary target at Leverkusen. Twenty aircraft are lost on the raid.

December 13 A total of 649 B-17s and B-24s bomb port areas of Bremen and Hamburg and U-boat yards at Kiel. This is the first mission in which more than 600 heavy bombers attack targets and, for the first time, P-51s escort the bombers.

December 20 For the first time VIII Bomber Command uses Window metal foil strips to confuse German radar-locating equipment.

ATTACKER'S CAPABILITIES
The American build-up

Leadership

The Commanding General of US Army Air Forces during 1943 was Henry "Hap" Arnold. Arnold was a supporter of Assistant Chief of Air Service Billy Mitchell, who advocated for an independent air force and saw strategic bombing as the unique thing that this air force could provide. Arnold was one of the "bomber generals" who paid little attention to fighter aviation, and in 1939 issued an order banning the development of external fuel tanks for tactical aircraft because of the fire hazard. However, he gradually came to believe that fighter aviation had been neglected.

For most of 1943, VIII Bomber Command was commanded by Arnold's friend Brigadier (later Major) General Ira Eaker, who, despite his background as a fighter pilot, was totally dedicated to the Air Corps Tactical School principle of daylight precision bombing without the need for fighter escorts. Eaker named Brigadier General Frank "Monk" Hunter head of VIII Fighter Command.

The first P-47Cs arrived in the United Kingdom in December 1942 and equipped the 4th Fighter Group. This picture was taken just after their arrival and before they had the white identification stripes applied. The P-47C was quickly replaced by the virtually identical P-47D, but engine and radio problems prevented the P-47 from being a factor in escorting bombers until the early summer. (NARA)

Bombers

B-17F

The main American heavy bomber in 1943 was the B-17F, designed for long-range, high-altitude – above 20,000ft – precision bombing and heavily armed since it would attack without fighter escort. The B-17 Flying Fortress was an excellent airplane, very tough and, even more important, easy to fly in the tight formations necessary to make German attacks more difficult. For normal combat missions deep into Germany, it carried a 4,000lb bomb load, usually eight 500lb bombs, though the types of bombs carried could vary considerably.

For the time, the ten-man crew of a B-17F carried a very heavy defensive armament, with up to 13 excellent .50-caliber Browning M2 machine guns with a rate of fire of approximately 800 rounds per minute, but they were not as effective as their number suggested. Six were

Getting into a ball turret on a B-17. The turret faced forward during take-off and landing, but for the gunner to bail out it had to point down so the hatch could be opened into the fuselage and the gunner could put on a parachute. The ball turret gunners' survival rate if the B-17 was hit was very low. (NARA)

very useful: two pairs of .50-caliber machine guns in two powered turrets, one on the top and one on the belly called the "ball turret," and a tail gun position with two .50-caliber machine guns on a pivot mount fired by a gunner whose position was kneeling on a bicycle seat.

There were two single-gun positions in the waist, but the guns were very heavy to maneuver, and the gunners had such a limited field of view that they were practically useless. Arguably these two crew members could have been dropped, which would have reduced personnel casualties by 20 percent.

Unfortunately, from November 1942 the Germans began to attack from the front, and there was a blind spot in front which neither the upper turret nor the ball turret could cover. The original B-17F had only one .30-caliber nose gun firing through one of four eyelets just off center, though that quickly changed as the head-on attacks began. Manually operated .50-caliber machine guns were mounted in the nose, but the nose was crowded, and the gun was manned by the bombardier, who was an officer and not a trained gunner.

For aircraft not being flown by lead crews, one forward gun modification that seemed effective was the addition of two .50-caliber guns mounted directly in the nose and protected by armor plate. The bombsight was removed, and it was manned by a trained enlisted gunner. These usually flew alongside the lead bomber to act as a type of escort.

The real solution was the powered Bendix chin turret that the YB-40 carried, and the last 86 Douglas-built B-17Fs had the chin turret fitted. This both increased the forward firepower and gave the bombardier more room. These modified B-17Fs were followed by the B-17G, in almost all ways identical to these late-model chin-turret B-17Fs.

Range was an important issue for the early B-17Fs. While the original B-17F's "official" combat range was 2,000 miles, this was a "straight line" out-and-back range, and for actual combat missions the radius was considerably less. After take-off, the bombers had to join in squadron formations, then fly a long, specified route to join with the group formations before proceeding to the target. All of these necessary maneuvers used fuel, which made the bombers' actual combat radius considerably less. This meant that for targets deep in Germany, the early B-17Fs could not fly diversionary routes and had to fly an almost straight line to the target, making the German fighter controllers' job much easier.

In May 1943, VIII Bomber Command began to receive late-production B-17Fs with "Tokyo tanks," additional fuel cells near the wing tips, providing another 1,080 gallons; this added considerably to their range, allowing them to fly diversionary routes. These modified B-17Fs were concentrated in one division, the 4th, which would be given the longest-distance raids. Unfortunately, the fuel sequence meant that the fuel in the "Tokyo tanks" was used early, and the fuel vapors remaining in the tanks made them prone to catch fire when they were hit.

B-24D Liberator

Two groups of B-24D Liberators arrived in England in 1942 and a third in June 1943, but about half of the B-24s were sent to North Africa between mid-December 1942 and late February 1943, to support Operation *Torch*, and several times the whole force was in North Africa. These deployed forces provided three of the five bomb groups used for the disastrous raid on the oil fields of Ploesti, Romania, Operation *Tidal Wave*, on August 1, 1943. Eighth Air Force B-24s were also a part of the very successful raid on August 13, 1943 against the Messerschmitt Bf 109 factory at Wiener Neustadt, one of the most heavily defended targets in Europe.

But, overall, the B-24 was a major disappointment in Europe. The B-24 had the same problem with head-on attacks as the B-17, but the B-24 had a very narrow nose so it could only carry a single .50-caliber center nose gun mounted to fire only in the horizontal plane. This armament left a blind spot which the upper turret could not cover. The B-24 was also unstable above 20,000ft and could not fly the close formations needed to counter Luftwaffe attacks. There were attempts to fly them in the same attacks with B-17s, but because of their different characteristics, especially speed, this proved impossible, and soon General Eaker began assigning the B-24s to tasks other than daylight bombing. The B-24s were also shuttled back and forth between Africa and England, and it was not until early September 1943 that

Virtually all the B-24s in VIII Bomber Command left in 1942 to support Operation *Torch*. Upon their return it was found that their performance was incompatible with that of the B-17 and they could not fly tight formations, so B-24s were only marginally effective for Eighth Air Force Bomber Command in 1943 but did yeoman service in North Africa and later Italy. (NARA)

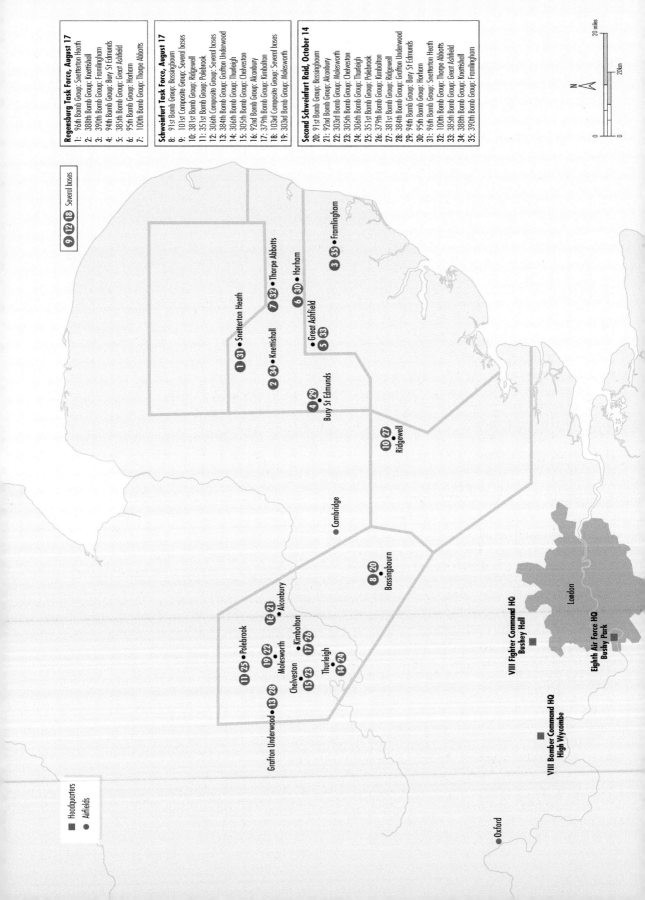

Regensburg Task Force, August 17
1: 96th Bomb Group: Snetterton Heath
2: 388th Bomb Group: Knettishall
3: 390th Bomb Group: Framlingham
4: 94th Bomb Group: Bury St Edmunds
5: 385th Bomb Group: Great Ashfield
6: 95th Bomb Group: Horham
7: 100th Bomb Group: Thorpe Abbotts

Schweinfurt Task Force, August 17
8: 91st Bomb Group: Bassingbourn
9: 101st Composite Group: Several bases
10: 381st Bomb Group: Ridgewell
11: 351st Bomb Group: Polebrook
12: 306th Composite Group: Several bases
13: 384th Bomb Group: Grafton Underwood
14: 306th Bomb Group: Thurleigh
15: 305th Bomb Group: Chelveston
16: 92nd Bomb Group: Alconbury
17: 379th Bomb Group: Kimbolton
18: 103rd Composite Group: Several bases
19: 303rd Bomb Group: Molesworth

Second Schweinfurt Raid, October 14
20: 91st Bomb Group: Bassingbourn
21: 92nd Bomb Group: Alconbury
22: 303rd Bomb Group: Molesworth
23: 305th Bomb Group: Chelveston
24: 306th Bomb Group: Thurleigh
25: 351st Bomb Group: Polebrook
26: 379th Bomb Group: Kimbolton
27: 381st Bomb Group: Ridgewell
28: 384th Bomb Group: Grafton Underwood
29: 94th Bomb Group: Bury St Edmunds
30: 95th Bomb Group: Horham
31: 96th Bomb Group: Snetterton Heath
32: 100th Bomb Group: Thorpe Abbotts
33: 385th Bomb Group: Great Ashfield
34: 388th Bomb Group: Knettishall
35: 390th Bomb Group: Framlingham

9 12 18 Several bases

Headquarters
Airfields

N

20 miles

20km

Oxford

VIII Bomber Command HQ
High Wycombe

VIII Fighter Command HQ
Bushey Hall

Eighth Air Force HQ
Bushey Park

London

Grafton Underwood
Polebrook
Molesworth
Chelveston
Kimbolton
Thurleigh
Alconbury

Cambridge

Bassingbourn

Ridgewell

Bury St Edmunds

Snetterton Heath

Knettishall

Thorpe Abbotts

Great Ashfield

Horham

Framlingham

the Eighth's three B-24 groups were back in England. A new group also arrived, bringing B-24 strength to four groups, while B-17 strength had increased to 16 combat groups, but the B-24s still made relatively little contribution to the CBO in 1943.

USAAF and RAF bombers compared

The B-17s and B-24s were designed from the start with characteristics that made them very different from the RAF's heavy bombers. RAF bombers attacked at night under the cover of darkness and had very modest defensive armament. Since they attacked single-ship, the ability to fly tight formation was not material, but maneuverability was. RAF bombers could perform almost fighter-like maneuvers to escape German night fighters. Also, RAF bombers had huge bomb bays and carried a much heavier bomb load, partly because they flew at relatively low altitudes.

Formations

It was quickly obvious to VIII Bomber Command that fighter attack would be the biggest threat to the American day bomber formations, so the bombers would have to fly in close formation for mutual support and to concentrate their firepower. But while these large numbers of bombers flying in formation would give adequate protection against fighter attacks, they would increase flak hazards and at the same time reduce accuracy by enlarging the resulting bomb pattern, since the formations bombed together.

There were many experiments trying to develop effective formations, but by late April 1943 VIII Bomber Command had developed a compact staggered formation that stacked low squadrons downward in one direction and high squadrons upward in the opposite direction. Later, a third element of three bombers was added to the 18-plane box, placed in the most exposed squadron for additional support. This resulted in a 21-plane wedge-shaped configuration that remained standard through September 1943.

To build an even larger formation for defense, three of the boxes were brought together into a "combat wing box," which covered a very large area roughly 2,000ft by 7,000ft – and there could be two or three combat wing boxes in a wedge-shaped formation if there were enough aircraft available. This was even more difficult to fly, but again there was no alternative.

The combat wing boxes usually flew in a column with 4–6 miles between each combat wing, with fighter escort when available above the boxes. However, if a combat wing lagged the escorts could lose visual contact, and if there was too much space the German controllers could see that and would attack the combat wing that was out of position.

There were many objections to such large and closely flown vertical formations, which were difficult to fly, unwieldy and very difficult to keep together, especially in turns. Turbulence from leading bombers added to the difficulty of maintaining formation. The lowermost and uppermost elements, trailing at the end of the formation, were in an exposed position and German fighters concentrated on them, with the result that the low squadron in the low group was called "Purple Heart Corner," after the decoration presented to wounded servicemen. Still, objectively, no matter what the formation, there was always going to be an outside corner that was more vulnerable than the center of the formation.

In the end the combat wing box's defensive firepower was deemed more important than maneuverability, and it was felt that the staggered "combat box" formation gave maximum fields of fire for mutual defensive support.

The top-secret Norden bombsight was expected to be the key to accurate daylight precision bombing, but with formation bombing in combat accuracy was not so necessary and it proved hard to use. It was almost replaced several times by a simpler sight. (NARA)

The key to success for a combat box was how tight the formation was – that usually determined whether or not the Germans attacked. A well-organized box with the groups and squadrons tight was not what the German controllers or attacking pilots were interested in attacking. They wanted disorganized formations, scattered and/or out of position.

Norden bombsight

One of the reasons the Air Corps committed to daylight precision bombing was the gyro-stabilized Norden M-4 bombsight, developed in the mid-1930s, ironically for the US Navy. The Air Corps ordered the Norden for its new B-17s, and tests of the Norden/B-17 combination – under ideal weather and visibility conditions – showed that it greatly exceeded the accuracy of its predecessors and would allow precision bombing from high altitude. The press fawned on the Norden, and to add to its mystique no photos were released and the details of how it worked remained top secret. However, the Norden was best when used by single aircraft that could maneuver to line up on the target independently. In combat, except for the few seconds of the bombing run, all phases of the bombing mission were dominated by considerations of defense, so the maneuvering necessary for the Norden to perform its best could not be met and the Norden bombsight, with its delicate adjustment, lost much of its value. The conditions that were best for both accuracy and protection from flak would not provide sufficient defense against fighter attacks in combat, and even under good conditions more than half the bombs hit more than 1,000ft from the target. At one point there was consideration of acquiring an inferior sight requiring less careful adjustment, a step which would seriously have compromised the ideal of precision which underlay the American bombardment theory.

Formation bombing and lead crews

Eighth Air Force Bomber Command had to develop procedures to strike the German targets with enough accuracy while keeping the bombers in their tight defensive formation. Additionally, while German fighters were the main threat, flak was a danger over the target. Flak handicapped effective bombing operations not so much by destroying or damaging bombers but rather by forcing the bombers to bomb at high altitudes, which reduced accuracy.

The German fighter defenses made it obvious that each bomber could not spread out and make its own bomb run, and as early as January 1943 formation bombing – entire formations dropping their bombs in unison when the lead bomber dropped his – was tried successfully. In March 1943 the Operational Research Section of VIII Bomber Command strongly recommended adopting this technique. In July 1943 VIII Bomber Command's leadership agreed, and ordered that the combat wings begin to plan to use formation bombing, despite the fact that it would be clumsy to maneuver the large formations onto the bombing run and that the resulting bomb pattern would scatter more widely than was the optimum for the desired accuracy.

To make formation bombing work, the wings needed well-coordinated teams of pilot, navigator, and bombardier, and these had to be developed. To that end, VIII Bomber Command directed the establishment of special "lead crews" in each squadron at each station. Squadrons had to identify their best bombardiers and they joined with a specially selected pilot and navigator. These lead crews alone would be responsible for identifying the target, leading the unit on the bomb run, locating the release point, and giving the order to release; and the lead crew pilot was chosen for his ability to fly smoothly and make changes gradually to keep the formation together. Only three other planes in each group – one wingman of the lead plane and the leaders of the high and low squadrons – carried bombsights, in case the leader was shot down. The mission of the other crews was to stay in tight defensive formation and release when the leader released.

The lead crews underwent intensive training so that they could act as group or squadron lead crews on combat missions. They often carried an additional navigator, and usually the tail gunner's position was occupied by an officer pilot who advised the pilot on the state of the formation. Finally, the lead crews were only to participate in combat as a lead crew, and their tour would be shortened by five missions. In addition to these crews, two very reliable B-17 aircraft in each squadron were designated as "lead bombers" and equipped with every approved device for accurate bombing of a target as it became available.

The critical moment in the entire mission was the few seconds immediately before the lead bombardier released the bombs, when he had to perform his final sighting operation and locate the bomb release point. This meant that the lead bomber had to be held as nearly as possible on a steady course without slips, skids, or changes in altitude, and VIII Bomber Command decided that a mechanical instrument could hold this precise position better

Head-on attacks by single-seat fighters began in November 1942 and were very effective, because American bombers had few forward guns and those they had were controlled by the bombardier, an officer who was not trained as a gunner. A field modification of dual .50-caliber machine guns was installed on some B-17s to provide extra firepower against head-on attacks. There was no bombsight with this modification because it was replaced by armor plate. These modified B-17s flew next to the lead bombers to provide extra firepower. (NARA)

than a pilot, who might be distracted by flak or attacking fighters. This automatic flight-control equipment (AFCE), an automatic pilot that regulated target approach and bomb run, was developed and first used successfully on March 18, 1943. The AFCE allowed the bombardier to control the aircraft on the bomb run with mechanical precision by the synchronized sighting and pilotage, and enabled him to provide a steadier bombing run than could be achieved even by veteran pilots. Soon all the specially designated "lead" B-17s received the AFCE.

Weather and radar bombing

The Luftwaffe was deadly, but the biggest impediment to VIII Bomber Command bombing was weather. Clouds split up combat wing boxes and dispersed the closely knit formations, and more importantly they could blanket targets, making it impossible to bomb. In desperation, in the late summer of 1943 VIII Bomber Command turned to the RAF, whose night bombers had a number of blind-bombing and navigational aids including *Gee*, a navigational aid using signals from ground stations, *Oboe*, a short-range precision navigation device, and *H2S*, an airborne radar scanner which showed a rough terrain image below the aircraft.

Both *Oboe* and *H2S* were in short supply and the RAF was reluctant to lend VIII Bomber Command these systems, ostensibly because of fear of them falling into enemy hands (though the RAF was losing dozens every night), but finally, in August 1943, both were given trial installations on B-17s. The *H2S* was preferred by VIII Bomber Command and several *H2S* systems were installed in the B-17's nose compartment, with the scanner encased in a large plastic bath under the nose. A special unit was formed to fly lead position in a combat wing with all bombers dropping on its release with British smoke marker bombs to mark the release point for following formations. Later, an American version of the *H2S*, the *H2X*, was brought into service.

Missions began on August 27, but were generally unsuccessful because of *H2S* failures and lack of training, and it was not until 1944 that *H2S* and its American equivalent, *H2X*, really became a part of VIII Bomber Command's arsenal.

A B-17's bomb bay was relatively small and its standard bomb load for long range missions into Germany was 4000 pounds. The RAF Avro Lancaster had a much larger bomb bay – 33ft unobstructed – and a normal bomb load was more than 14,000lb. The Lancaster was also faster and more manoeuvrable but lightly armed and flew at much lower altitudes. (NARA)

A P-38F Lightning carrying two external fuel tanks between the fuselage and engines. This doubled the P-38's range to close to that of a B-17, but they were all sent to Africa for Operation *Torch* in late 1942/early 1943 and missed the battles of the fall of 1943 where they would have been very effective against the German twin-engine rocket fighters. However, the German single-seat fighters were much superior. (NARA)

Fighter escorts

For a time in late 1942, some Eighth Air Force officers believed that the American heavy bombers could fight their way through German fighter opposition. But their hopes died out as the missions over Germany in early 1943 began to run into stiff resistance, and as the spring and summer campaigns progressed it became increasingly evident that some sort of escort would be required if daylight strategic bombing was to be successful.

There were initially two candidates for VIII Fighter Command: the large P-47 Thunderbolt and the even larger twin-engine P-38 Lightning. Both were designed as fast-climbing, high-altitude bomber interceptors with powerful turbo-supercharged engines. Because of this limited mission, they also had very short range on internal fuel, both carrying about 300 gallons, and the P-47 had no provision for carrying external fuel tanks.

P-38 Lightning

In June 1942 the first P-38F Lightning arrived in England. The Lightning had shackles mounted between the engine and fuselage to carry 150-gallon drop tanks for ferry purposes. The tanks doubled the amount of fuel the P-38 carried and allowed it to fly all the way to England, with several stops, and in the summer of 1942 186 P-38s flew from the United States to the United Kingdom.

The P-38s flew their first combat missions on September 2, 1942, but as the only really capable American fighter in the United Kingdom in any numbers, from October 1942 they were all assigned to become part of Operation *Torch*, the Allied invasion of North Africa in November 1942. By the end of 1942 virtually all of the P-38s had left the United Kingdom for North Africa, and VIII Fighter Command was without fighters until early 1943.

This decision to send the P-38s to North Africa proved to be an especially short-sighted decision. It reflected the prewar Tactical School/USAAF position that unescorted bomber formations could survive against heavy fighter opposition, but this showed a fundamental misunderstanding of the situation over Germany. With external tanks, the P-38F had a

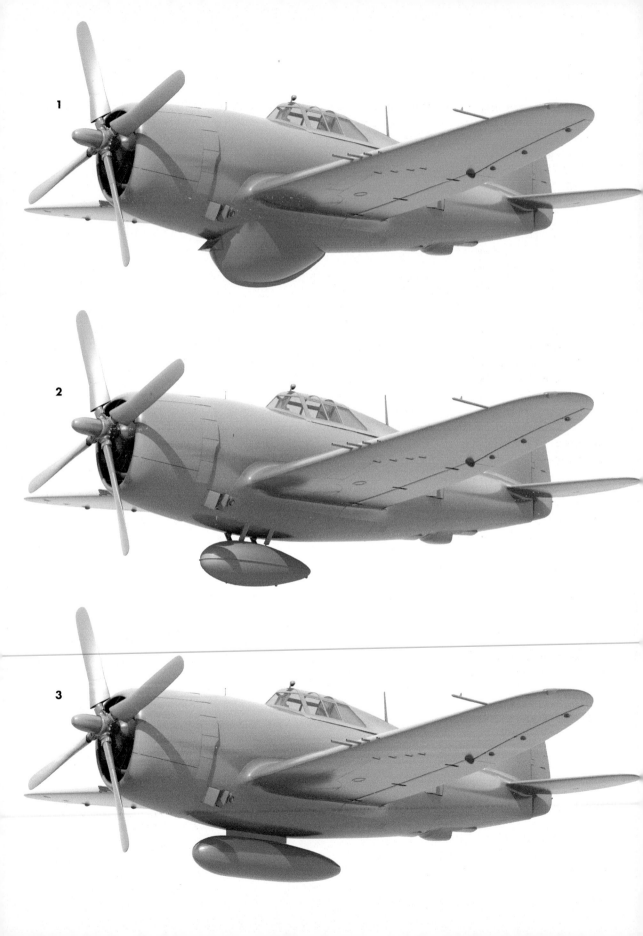

OPPOSITE: P-47 EXTERNAL TANKS

1: The first P-47 external tank used was a 200-gallon resonated ferry tank attached to the P-47 with four suspension points. The tank usually carried only 100 gallons, and being unpressurized the fuel could not be used above 20,000ft. The tank was very difficult to jettison cleanly so some tanks had a wedge on the front of the tank to push the nose of the tank down when it was jettisoned. In early July there were 1,100 of these tanks in England, and it added about 75 miles to the combat radius of the P-47.

2: The 75-gallon metal tank (actually, it carried 85 gallons) was developed for the P-39 Airacobra and was adapted for use on the P-47. It had much less drag than the 200-gallon tank and it could be pressurized. It began to arrive at the end of August.

3: The P-47s also used the British 108-gallon paper tank, which was made by wrapping layers of resorcinol glue-impregnated paper around a cylinder to give the center portion its shape. The glue would slowly dissolve from the solvent effects of the fuel inside, developing leaks within a few hours of being loaded, making them a strictly one-time use item, filled right before takeoff. On October 4 these tanks allowed P-47s to shoot down ten Bf 110s. Some P-47s had a fairing around the mount for streamlining.

combat radius of over 500 miles, and P-38s could have easily escorted the B-17s deep into Germany to Schweinfurt, Regensburg, and other targets. Whatever the P-38's performance shortcomings (and there were many), it would have been an effective counter to the deadly twin-engine Bf 110 and Me 410 *Zerstörer* that decimated B-17 formations in the second half of 1943. What the bombers needed was not fighters with the performance to defeat the Bf 109s or Fw 190s, but those with the range to meet and counter the *Zerstörer*.

The P-38s returned to the United Kingdom in the late fall of 1943 just after the second raid on Schweinfurt and made a small contribution as an escort in early 1944, but they are worthy of mention because of this one great "what if."

P-47 Thunderbolt

The fighter that did carry the escort load in 1943, the P-47 Thunderbolt, began to arrive in the United Kingdom in late December 1942. The first P-47 group, the 4th Fighter Group, turned in their Spitfires and became operational with the P-47 in early March 1943, but they were not impressed. In April 1943 the P-47 was tested against the Fw 190, and the tests found that while the Thunderbolt showed exceptional performance above 20,000ft because of its turbo-supercharger, the 60ft of air ducting for the supercharger and the Thunderbolt's

The P-47D was tested against an Fw 190 captured by the RAF in April 1943 after the P-47 had solved its radio and engine problems. The Fw 190 was superior below 20,000ft, but the P-47 better above because of its turbo-supercharged engine. But they were fairly closely matched and the outcome of a dogfight would depend on the skill of the pilots. (NARA)

The first P-47 external fuel tank was a 200-gallon unpressurized paper ferry tank. They were brought to England in the spring of 1943 but were not put into service until late July 1943. They had many problems – only about 100 gallons were useable and because they were unpressurized they could not be employed above 20,000ft – but they added about 75 miles to the P-47's range and were a nasty shock to the Luftwaffe. (NARA)

heavy weight gave it poor acceleration, and the Focke-Wulf outclimbed and outmaneuvered it easily. When the P-47s first began to fly combat missions, they rarely engaged German fighters so the maintenance teams had a chance to solve the Thunderbolt's early problems with radios and the pilots had an opportunity to develop escort tactics. This allowed them to gain both confidence and experience without heavy combat.

Once they began to escort American bombers, the P-47 groups' tactics made them a favorite of the bomber crews. The RAF Spitfires flew at very high altitude, where they outperformed the German fighters, but were often too late to prevent the initial German attack. The P-47s flew the three squadrons of the group above the bombers, with the center squadron 2,000–3,000ft above the others, which in turn flew 3,000–4,000ft higher than the bombers. The center and highest squadron acted as "top cover" protection for the lower squadrons, whose job it was to intercept enemy fighters making for the bombers. This gave the Germans the initiative, but also ensured that they would be intercepted prior to their first pass.

The P-47's major limitation was range. Its 2,000hp Pratt & Whitney engine used fuel rapidly – 100 gallons per hour on a combat mission, whereas the standard RAF fighter, the Spitfire IX, used 45 gallons per hour – giving it a combat radius of action of less than 200 miles. It was this range limitation that made the P-47 ineffective for the first half of 1943, but the introduction of various types of jettisonable external fuel tanks beginning in late July allowed the Thunderbolts to extend their combat radius somewhat so they could escort the bombers and keep the rocket-firing German Zerstörer at bay. However, they still were range-limited and the German controllers quickly recalibrated to keep the rocket fighters out of their range.

P-47 external tanks

The use of external fuel tanks was the most important tactical development for VIII Fighter Command, but their long-delayed development and deployment was a sad story that cost many American bomber crewmen their lives, the result of the flawed doctrine of the self-protecting bomber promulgated by the Air Corps Tactical School.

The idea of external fuel tanks was not new – the Army Air Corps had experimented with external fuel tanks for tactical aircraft in the late 1930s – but in May 1939 General Arnold, a product of the Air Corps Tactical School, issued an order forbidding their use because of a suspected fire hazard. However, when the war began, and the USAAF was faced with

the problem of moving fighters long distances, General Arnold modified his position. On February 20, 1942 he authorized the development and manufacture of external fuel tanks for fighters. An unpressurized paper 200-gallon belly "bath-tub" for the P-47 began to arrive in theater in March, but it was only intended for ferry purposes and jettisoning the tanks was difficult and intended only for emergencies. The P-47 groups also found that only 100 of the advertised 200 gallons were really usable, and since the tanks were unpressurized the fuel would not feed above 20,000ft. The tanks also barely cleared the ground on grass airfields. But heavy losses in unescorted bomber formations forced VIII Fighter Command to load the unpressurized 200-gallon tanks as an interim measure. By early July over 1,100 of these were in the United Kingdom, and even with their limitations the three P-47 groups began to use the tanks in late July 1943, and the 75-mile range increase was a nasty surprise for the Luftwaffe.

Unfortunately, the development and production of suitable drop tanks proved very difficult, particularly on the American side. While some in Washington recognized the importance of these range-extending tanks, there was a lack of communication between Eighth Air Force and procurement officials at home. Back in the United States they mistakenly believed that production in Britain could meet Eighth Air Force's needs. In the United Kingdom, Eighth Air Force negotiated a deal with the British Ministry of Aircraft Production for 60,000 108-gallon metal external tanks; however, General Eaker paid little attention because external fuel tanks were only his number four priority, and he did not

By September the P-47 groups finally had enough of several different types of pressured external fuel tanks to reach into Germany. These P-47s are carrying a metal 75-gallon tank originally used on the P-39 Aircobra. (NARA)

The struggle to get useable external fuel tanks to increase the range of the P-47 escorts was a long and sad story. Here is a P-47 with a British-made 108-gallon tank, which finally became available in September 1943. (NARA)

The YB-40 was a converted B-17F with added armament, including dual waist guns and an extra power turret in the radio compartment. It also had a turret below the nose, a modification that was successfully adopted by later B-17s. The YB-40 was not successful because it had poor flying characteristics and most of its armament was not useful in the front quarter, from where the Germans mostly attacked. It was a favorite of General Eaker, who was not enthusiastic about single seat fighter escort. This brought him into conflict with the Commander of the Army Air Force General "Hap" Arnold. (NARA)

give the Ministry of Aircraft Production clear orders until the first week of October, so very few were produced. The bomber losses continued to soar, leading VIII Fighter Command to order a 108-gallon RAF paper composition tank, originally designed for ferrying RAF Hawker Hurricane IIs. Finally, at the beginning of September 1943, the first British-made 108-gallon steel tanks and 108-gallon paper tanks became operational. The P-47s first used them on their September 27 mission to Emden, even though there was only 4in ground clearance under these tanks and they could not be used on "rough" airfields. VIII Fighter Command also ordered 75-gallon all-steel teardrop-shaped centerline fuel tanks designed for the P-39 fighter. They were shipped at great cost to the United Kingdom and modified for use on the P-47 in late August after the Schweinfurt–Regensburg raids; they proved very effective.

On October 14, Eaker contacted the Ministry of Aircraft Production to complain of shortfalls in drop tank production and suggested that of 30 bombers lost over Münster on the 10th, the availability of drop tanks might have saved as many as 20. The Ministry pointed out that only in June had Eighth Air Force sought large numbers of workable drop tanks and the USAAF did not give British industry approval for the required fittings until early October.

YB-40

When America entered the war there was real doubt about the technical feasibility of developing a truly long-range escort fighter. The RAF and Luftwaffe thought it was impossible (though the Japanese Zero had a range of over 1,200 miles), but in mid-1942 the USAAF began to consider that the Tactical School doctrine of the self-protecting bomber formations might be flawed, and in September 1942 the Army Air Force converted a B-17F into an "escort fighter" for a formation defense role. Designated the YB-40, it had two additional power turrets, one over the radio room and one in a remotely controlled installation under the nose, and dual manually operated gun positions replaced single guns in waist windows, giving the aircraft a total of 14 .50 caliber machine guns. It also carried much more ammunition and additional armor plate around the crew stations.

Eaker was enthusiastic about the YB-40 idea, much more so than about increasing the range of Eighth Air Force's fighters with external tanks, and in May 1943 13 experimental models were sent to the 327th Squadron, 92nd Group for combat trials. For two months, from late May 1943 through late July 1943, YB-40s flew combat missions, but it proved to be an abject failure. The YB-40 was too heavy to keep up with normal B-17 formations after they dropped their bombs, and while it had more guns, they fired mostly to the side and were of little help since most Luftwaffe passes were from the front or rear. The most troublesome aspect of the YB-40 was its flying characteristics, particularly its tendency to fly tail-heavy due to the added weight in the rear section. On many missions, YB-40s flew in the "Purple Heart Corner" also known as the "coffin corner," but after a few missions it was clear they would not be the solution to the escort issue. However, the chin turret of the YB-40 proved very effective and was quickly adopted for late-model B-17Fs and for the B-17G.

DEFENDER'S CAPABILITIES
The Luftwaffe in 1943

Origins

The Luftwaffe was, when compared to the USAAF and RAF, a very young force, officially re-established in February 1935 (though German pilots had been training in Russia since the 1920s). The new Luftwaffe was very different from the German Air Force of World War I, which had placed a heavy emphasis on strategic bombing of England with large and capable bombers and Zeppelins. Ironically, this campaign was the impetus for the British to form the RAF as an independent arm for strategic bombing, and the independent RAF was the model for the US Air Corps Tactical School developing strategic bombing doctrine to eventually lead to an independent United States Air Force.

Some early Luftwaffe leaders wanted to develop a strategic bombing capability, but that was expensive and the German General Staff had a new type of war in mind, the fast-moving *Blitzkrieg*, so the Luftwaffe was mainly dedicated to tactical air power using fighters and fast medium-bombers to destroy enemy air power in the battle zone, along with pinpoint dive bombing to support the army's rapid thrusts. These concepts were buttressed by the successful Luftwaffe participation from 1936 to 1939 in the Spanish Civil War under the name of the Condor Legion. The Spanish Civil War also gave the Luftwaffe much more current combat experience than the RAF and USAAF, and this served the Luftwaffe well from the beginning through to the middle of the war.

Leadership

Reichsmarschall Hermann Göring, a Hitler favorite and World War I ace, was the commander-in-chief of the Luftwaffe and his control over all aspects of aviation was absolute. Göring left the organization and building of the Luftwaffe to Erhard Milch, his deputy and Air Inspector General in charge of aircraft production, while Albert Speer had the position of Reich Minister of Armaments and War Production. In November 1941 the 39-year-old

The most effective German day fighter was the tough Focke-Wulf Fw 190A-6, shown here carrying the standard 80-gallon external tank to increase its range. (Bundesarchiv, Bild 1011-736-0180-13, Fotograf: o.Ang.)

Airfleet headquarters
Airfleet boundary
Air Division headquarters
Air Division headquarters
Maximum range of escort fighters

NORWAY

SWEDEN

DENMARK

North Sea

Baltic Sea

NETHERLANDS

**JAGDFLIEGERFÜHRER
DEUTSCHE BUCHT**

■ ● Hamburg
Jagddivision 2

▲■ ● Berlin
Luftwaffen Befehlshaber Mitte
Jagddivision 4

GREAT BRITAIN

● London

■ ● Deelen
Jagddivision 1

**JAGDFLIEGERFÜHRER
HOLLAND-RUHRGEBIET**

**JAGDFLIEGERFÜHRER
BERLIN-MITTELDEUTSCHLAND**

● Cologne

BELGIUM

● Frankfurt

● Schweinfurt

BOHEMIA &
MORAVIA

LUX.

P-47 ● - ■ ● Metz
Jagddivision 3

GERMANY

● Regensburg

▲ ● Paris
Luftflotte 3

Schleissheim
Jagddivision 5
■ ● Munich

FRANCE

AUSTRIA

P-47 with drop tank

SWITZERLAND

YUGOSLAVIA

ITALY

P-38 with drop tanks

N

0   200 miles
0   200km

OPPOSITE GERMAN FIGHTER DEFENSES 1943

Adolf Galland became commander of the German fighter force (General der Jagdflieger), despite having no staff experience. It was a frustrating job for the 96-victory ace, but despite his lack of experience, Galland – who always saw himself as a combat leader and not wanting to be "tied to a desk job" – acquitted himself well.

The Luftwaffe Chief of the General Staff was Generaloberst Hans Jeschonnek, who was mainly focused on the offensive capabilities of the Luftwaffe in the East and Mediterranean, but when the American daylight raids began, Milch and Galland wanted to build up the defenses in Germany itself. They were concerned from the start about American bombing because it could hit industrial targets accurately, and Milch especially was very aware of all of German industry's choke points. As the RAF night raids and expanding American day raids demanded more defensive air power, Göring and Hitler – who took an active if intermittent interest in the Luftwaffe – made Jeschonnek's life miserable and eventually drove him to suicide. Generaloberst Günther Korten replaced him on August 25, 1943, and reorganized the Luftwaffe with its primary mission being the defense of Germany. This shift in emphasis was especially effective against American daylight bombing; and the losses it caused, combined with bad weather, were mainly responsible for the German victory over VIII Bomber Command in the fall of 1943.

German fighters

To counter the American day bombing campaign in 1943, the Reichs-Luftverteidigung (RLV) day-fighter organization initially relied on two single-engine fighters, the Messerschmitt Bf 109F/G and the Focke-Wulf Fw 190A-6 single-engine fighters. These were joined in August 1943 by what were to be the RLV's most effective weapons against the bombers, the twin-engine *Zerstörer* (destroyers), the Messerschmitt Bf 110G and Me 410A. The day fighters were supplemented by heavily armed Bf 110G night fighters, though these were valuable assets and the backbone of the German night fighter force, so they had to be kept well beyond the range of the escort fighters.

Two things proved very helpful for RLV fighters as the campaign progressed. All German fighter aircraft had provisions for *Rüstsätze*, field modifications packaged in kit form direct from the aircraft manufacturer, and these allowed rapid fitting of new heavy weapons on German fighters. Additionally, unlike American fighters which struggled to find proper external fuel tanks for much of 1943, from the beginning all German fighters could carry the standard Luftwaffe jettisonable external 80-gallon fuel tank, which allowed them extra range, though from time to time these were in short supply.

Single-engine fighters

The most effective RLV single-engine fighter was the Fw 190A-6, mainly because of its heavy built-in armament – four 20mm cannon and two 7.92mm machine guns – and its large, tough BMW 801 radial engine which could often absorb American .50-caliber bullets. The small 7.92mm machine guns were soon replaced by 13mm guns, and the Fw 190 could also carry a large variety of extra *Rüstsätze* weapons, such as two Werfer-Granate 21 (Wfr. Gr. 21) rocket tubes or extra underwing cannon, with relatively little drop-off in performance.

The other German single-engine fighter was the smaller Bf 109F/G. It had similar performance to the Fw 190 but was better at high altitude; however, its built-in armament was only a single 20mm cannon mounted in the propeller hub and two cowl-mounted 7.92mm machine guns. The Bf 109's small size and thin wing made it harder to add additional

A Bf 109 with two Wfr. Gr. 21 rocket launchers under the wing. The light, thin-winged Bf 109 was unsuited for extra armament but it was a large part of the German day fighter force and had to take part in the battles against American bombers. (Bundesarchiv, Bild 1011-469-1481-07A, Fotograf: o.Ang)

armament; for the anti-bomber role many Bf 109s were equipped with a *Rüstsätze* of two Wfr. Gr. 21 tubes or two extra 20mm cannon in underwing pods, but both dramatically reduced performance. A more useful weapon was the 30mm Mk 108 cannon, a factory replacement mounted in the propeller hub on one model, the Bf 109G/U4. Later Bf 109s also had the cowl-mounted 7.92mm machine guns replaced by 13mm guns.

Twin-engine fighters

By far the most successful fighters against the American bombers were the twin-engine fighters, known as *Zerstörer*, the Messerschmitt Bf 110G and Me 410A. Surprisingly, no effort was made to use these twin-engine day fighters for the daylight air defense mission until American bomber attacks increased in the summer of 1943, and then Bf 110 and Me 410 units were called back to the Reich from the Eastern Front and Mediterranean.

The heavily armed Bf 110, shown here with four rocket pods and two extra 30mm cannon in a belly tray, was an extremely effective bomber killer but helpless against single-seat fighters, as had been shown as early as the Battle of Britain. (Bundesarchiv 1011-649-5369-01, Fotograf: Hausmann)

The Bf 110 had had a checkered career. It had been unsuccessful as a day fighter during the Battle of Britain but later served with distinction in the Mediterranean and in Russia in a variety of roles, including those of heavy escort fighter, light bomber, close air support, and reconnaissance. By the end of 1941, Bf 110G production had slowed while waiting for its designated successor, the Me 210, but the Me 210 was an abject failure, and for lack of a suitable replacement the Bf 110G went back in full production in 1942. Beginning in the summer

The explosions from a Wfr. Gr. 21. The frag pattern was over 100ft so it was unnecessary to hit a bomber to damage it. (NARA)

of 1943, the day fighter version was brought back from Russia and the Mediterranean, and modified with a variety of heavy weapons to attack USAAF bombers.

The Me 210's replacement, the Me 410, had much-improved performance and began to enter service in January 1943. The Me 410 could carry an even larger number of weapons than the Bf 110G, including the long-barreled Bk-5 50mm cannon.

The Bf 110's and Me 410's endurance allowed them to make multiple continuous attacks against unescorted USAAF bomber formations, which the Germans called *Pulks*, and their ability to carry a variety of heavy cannon and missiles made them deadly weapons. However, they were unmaneuverable and helpless if they were caught by escort fighters.

Weapons

When the RLV fighters began to encounter the tough American bombers, especially the B-17s, it quickly became clear to the German fighter pilots that they needed heavier armament. Galland, the former fighter pilot, took a very hands-on approach to try to defeat the American heavy bombers, and after talking to the pilots about their lack of firepower he established an operational test unit, Erprobungskommando 25 (Test Unit 25, or ErprKdo 25), to develop cannon, air-to-air missiles, and anything else they could imagine to counter the bombers.

The unit tried every idea they could come up with. They tried unsuccessfully to lay parachute-retarded "minefields" in the path of the American bomber *Pulks* and to drop time-fuzed bombs on them, but aiming both proved impossible. Another weapon that ErprKdo 25 tried was the 73mm RZ 65 rocket carried in a streamlined container on the Bf 109F. The container had little effect on performance, but the rockets were too small to be effective even if they hit, so after a period of combat tests it was dropped.

Rüstsätze with additional heavy cannon were useful, but the most promising weapon was the Wfr. Gr. 21 rocket, used by the German Army's 21cm Nebelwerfer 42 infantry multiple rocket launcher. This was a large, solid fuel spin-stabilized rocket with a 90lb warhead, with a lethal blast area of approximately 100ft and a range of over half a mile, well out of

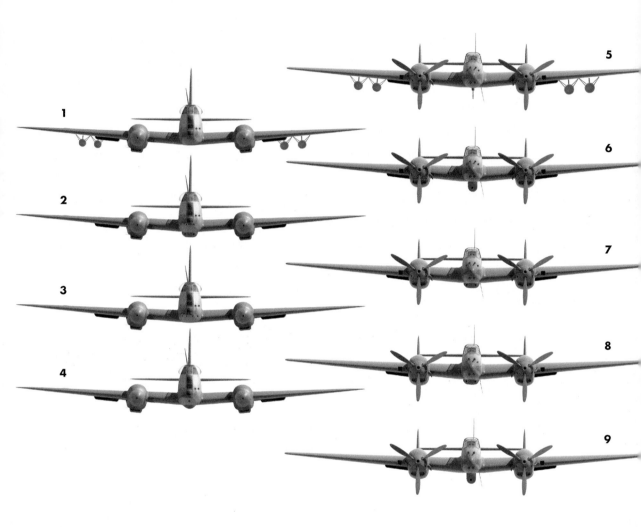

LUFTWAFFE FIGHTER ARMAMENT

1. Messerschmitt Me 410A-1/U-2 *Hornesse*
Basic forward firing armament 4x 7.92mm machine guns
and 4x MG 151/20 20mm cannon
All could carry four Wfr. Gr. 21 rocket launchers, two under
each wing

2: Me 410A-1/U-2/*Rüstsätze 4*
2x MG 151/20 in forward weapons bay
2x MG 151/20 in a ventral tray

3: Me 410A-1/U-2/ *Rüstsätze 2*
4x MG 151/20 in weapons bay

4: Me 410B-2/U-4
Single 50mm cannon in weapons bay – not a *Rüstsätze*

5. Messerschmitt Bf 110G-2
Basic armament: 4x MG 81 7.92mm machine guns and
two MG 151/20 cannon
All could carry four Wfr. Gr. 21 rocket launchers

6: Bf 110G-2/*Rüstsätze 1*
37mm BK 3.7 cannon in fairing on centerline

7: Bf 110G-2/*Rüstsätze 2*
Two extra MG 151/20s in tray under fuselage

8: Bf 110G-2/*Rüstsätze 3* nose machine guns replaced
by 2x 30mm Mk 108 cannon plus 2x MG 151/20 in a
tray like the R2

9: Bf 110G-2/*Rüstsätze 4* The 37mm Bk 3.7 cannon plus
the two 30mm Mk 108 cannon as in R3

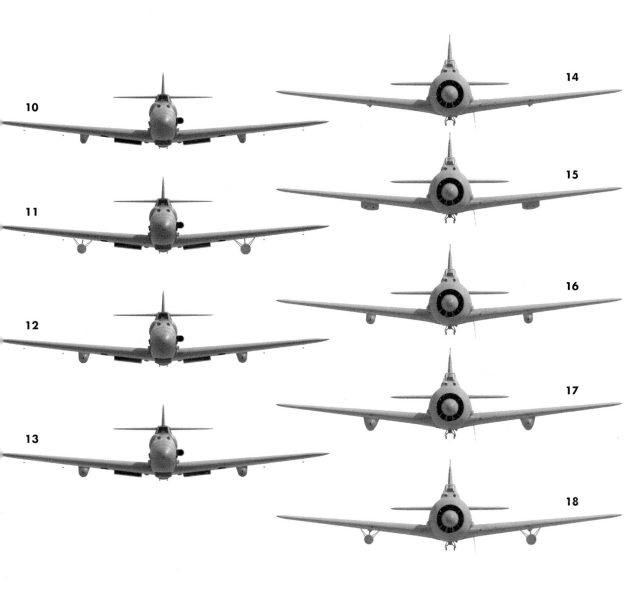

10. Messerschmitt Bf 109G-6
Built-in armament: 1x MG 151 20mm cannon in the propeller hub and two 13mm MG 131 machine guns, one on each side above the engine. Wiring for *Rüstsätze* underwing cannon gondolas and other *Rüstsätze* was added from the first of the G-6 series production.
11: G-6/ *Rüstsätze* 2
Two Wfr. Gr. 21 rocket launchers
12: G-6/ *Rüstsätze* 4
Two MK 108 30mm cannon in underwing gondolas
13: G-6/ *Rüstsätze* 6
Two MG 151/20 in underwing gondolas

14. Focke-Wulf Fw 190A-8
Built-in armament: 2x MG 17 7.92mm machine guns, two MG FF 20mm cannon, two MG 151/20mm cannon
15: A-8/ *Rüstsätze* 1
Four MG-151/20s
16: A-8/ *Rüstsätze* 2 replaced the outer wing 20mm cannon with a 30mm MK 108 cannon
17: A-8/ *Rüstsätze* 3 gondola and long-barrel MK 103 30mmm cannon
18: A-8/ *Rüstsätze* 6 Two Wfr. Gr. 21 rocket launchers

A B-17 is blown to bits by a direct hit from a Wfr. Gr. 21 rocket. (NARA)

reach of the bombers' defensive .50-caliber guns. The rocket was fitted into a rifled, braced "stovepipe" tube carried under a fighter's wing, and the rocket and launch tube weighed about 250lb. While the Wfr. Gr. 21 had long range, it had a low launch velocity, which created a significant ballistic drop. To get the range necessary to hit a co-altitude bomber formation, the missile had to be "lobbed" at the target, so the launch tube had to be mounted at a roughly 15-degree angle upwards from the wing line. This produced a great deal of drag that inhibited the fighter's performance, but the increased firepower made it worthwhile. The tube could be jettisoned if necessary, but the jettison mechanism was unreliable.

A time-fuze detonated the warhead at a pre-set distance from the launch point, and the rocket took from four to five seconds to travel this distance. It was usually fired at the center of the bomber *Pulk*, so if it fell short or went long it would explode inside the formation.

Since the rocket was not accurate enough to hit a single bomber, the tactic was to have a large formation of rocket fighters fly behind a bomber formation and make a simultaneous mass rocket launch into the bomber formation from outside the range of the defensive guns. The rocket's huge blast radius compensated for inaccuracy, and the explosions were expected to make the bombers take evasive maneuvers that would break up the formation enough for the single-engine fighters to make their head-on attacks with cannon.

The Bf 109s and Fw 190s of coastal units were the first front-line units to get the Wfr. Gr. 21 and began firing it in July 1943. They were effective and made a real impression on the American bomber crews, but the single-seat fighters could only carry two missiles and the drag of the weapons caused a large decrease in performance. The real breakthrough came on August 2, 1943, when the RLV directed that the newly arrived Bf 110 and Me 410 *Zerstörer* should be fitted with four Wfr. Gr. 21 launchers, two under each wing. On August 15 the first Bf 110G-2 was fitted with the weapons, and the rest of the Bf 110s and Me 410s followed. The single-seat units continued to carry them, one flight per *Staffel* (squadron).

Initial tactics

Attacking the American heavy bombers required new attack methods, and the *Gruppenkommandeur* (group commander) of the 3rd Staffel of Jagdgeschwader 2 (III./

JG 2), Hauptmann Egon Mayer, and his staff developed the idea of head-on attacks on the bomber formations. The tactic was to fly parallel to and then well to the front of the bomber formation, climb above them, then turn as a group and from a 10-degree dive make a mass head-on attack. The tactic was first used in November 1942 and proved very effective, because the cannon-fire from a head-on pass hit the American bombers in their most vulnerable spot, the engines and pilot crew compartment, where there were few guns. Mayer passed the tactic to his headquarters and this became the standard method for single-engine fighters to attack heavy bomber formations.

There were, however, disadvantages to making mass head-on attacks on the American bombers. The tactic required the attacker to press to very close range on the bomber formations and that was a challenge, even for the best German fighter pilots. It took a high degree of skill, a cool head, and iron nerves to face the storm of defensive fire and still press home such attacks. Even if the German fighters slowed as they came in, the pass generated closing speeds of 500mph and there was only a short time available to line up and fire. For that reason, the head-on pass was not always used, especially when the unit had a number of inexperienced pilots, and in fact some German pilots simply did not have the stomach for such close-range combat and developed *Viermotschreck* (fear of the four-engine bombers); this was a problem throughout the campaign.

Pilots

By the beginning of 1943, training of new German pilots was beginning to become an issue, and in February basic pilot training was reduced from 72 to 52 weeks because of a shortage of aviation fuel. From that point on, single-seat fighter pilots had less training but, on the whole, General der Flieger Werner Kreipe, chief of Luftwaffe training, was satisfied with progress throughout 1943: "The needs of the front have been met." This was to prove false, but did not become a real issue until 1944.

Another problem was the same one that the Americans had: weather. The Americans flew over the weather in Germany, while the Germans had to fly through it on both take-off and landing. German single-engine fighter pilots, especially new ones, had problems flying in bad weather, and there were many accidents which cost aircraft as well as pilots; some sources say that in 1943 the RLV lost as many fighters and pilots to accidents as they did to the Americans.

Aircraft numbers

German single-seat fighter losses were soaring as 1943 progressed, especially in the losing battles in the Mediterranean, and there was a consistent stream of heavy losses on the Eastern Front. While there was some sentiment for developing improved fighters, Milch, and to a lesser extent Galland, realized that it was numbers that mattered, not incremental increases in performance. Speer was able to increase fighter production so much that the numbers of fighters rose in 1943 from a little over 1,300 at the end of 1942 to over 2,000 at the end of September 1943. The increase, combined with the moves of single- and twin-engine fighters back to defend Germany, allowed an increase in fighter strength even with the heavy losses that were being suffered. In Germany proper, the Luftwaffe's defense had grown from a single *Jagdgeschwader* with fewer than 100 aircraft in January 1943 to 11 *Jagdgeschwader* with 20 assigned groups in September 1943.

Reaction to American daylight strategic attacks

In 1942 and early in 1943, central Germany was almost undefended because there was a huge demand for fighters for the Eastern and Mediterranean fronts, as well as daily RAF fighter-bomber raids along the European northwest coast. The German air defenses in the west had only two *Jagdgeschwader*, about 145 fighters, on the northeast French, Dutch, and

German coasts. Because they were in constant combat with RAF raids on the coast, even with their small number these wings were considered the most skillful in the Luftwaffe and through 1942 had the situation well in hand.

The small, escorted US heavy bomber raids that began in August 1942 were quickly noticed by German fighter pilots on the coast, who realized that attacking American bombers packed with heavy machine guns was a different game than attacking lightly armed RAF attack aircraft.

At the beginning of 1943, both Galland and Milch warned Göring that the buildup of American bombers was an existential threat, especially with the American mass production capability, and that the German air defenses had little depth. At first their warnings were ignored, and German weapon procurement priorities put fighters low on the list. Fortunately for the advocates of Reich defense, events of the war slowly changed the RLV force structure. Beginning in February 1943, fighter units began to be transferred back from Russia, and in the spring German fighter production began to increase dramatically as priorities were rearranged. When the Mediterranean Front collapsed, more fighters were moved to Germany and, after the massive defeat on the Eastern Front at Kursk, the Luftwaffe high command downgraded close air support and moved more and more fighters back to Germany. By June 1943, when the US Eighth Air Force began to fly serious unescorted missions into northwestern Germany, the Luftwaffe had increased the number of fighters on the Western Front from 350 to almost 600, with more coming in.

Command and control

When VIII Bomber Command began to fly into Germany, the German air defense system was the best in the world, far better than the British system during the Battle of Britain. The Luftwaffe day fighter command and control system organization had access to the sophisticated radar network built up to counter RAF night bombers, but RAF bombers did not fly in formation and shooting them down was basically a single fighter stalking a single bomber. The large formations of American raids presented a different problem for the day fighters, and it quickly became clear that success against the large, tight American daylight bomber formations would depend on a concentration of a large number of fighters with heavy weapons acting in concert. This was the goal of the RLV day fighter command and control system.

Signals intelligence

American bombing raids inevitably generated a large volume of radio traffic, especially when preparing to launch a large mission, and these communications provided the earliest warning of the raids. This traffic was intercepted by the Luftwaffe's listening and intercept service, the Funkhorchdienst ("Y-Service" or H-Dienst), which worked closely with early warning radar stations to predict the raid's likely route and targets in order to begin forming an accurate picture of the air situation.

Fühlungshalter

A very important part of the Luftwaffe command and control system was information from airborne *Fühlungshalter* "contact keepers," a special *Staffel* of eight to ten long-range bombers assigned to shadow the bomber formations and pass all the pertinent information, including escort status, to the ground controllers. They became a familiar sight to USAAF bomber crews on deep penetrations into Germany, and the American crews believed – incorrectly – that these aircraft issued orders directly to the formation leaders in the air.

Radar

In 1943, the *Jagdkorps* (fighter corps) and *Jagddivisionen* (fighter divisions) depended on *Freya* early warning radars with a range of about 90 miles, combined with *Würzburg* tracking radars

that provided altitude information. In the middle of 1943, the *Freya/Würzburg* combination was augmented by a new generation of more powerful and sophisticated radar equipment, notably the FuMG 41/42 *Mammut*, a long-range early warning radar, the world's first three-dimensional radar that used a phased array for beam deflection, with a range of about 170 miles.

While radar was critical, in clear weather the *Flugwache*, a network of ground observers, performed a vital role, filling radar gaps and providing valuable information because they could identify aircraft types and provide visual reports to update the air situation picture.

Tracking the raid

As a raid developed, the *Jagdkorps* operations room controllers, initially in Deelen, Holland, formed an early picture of the raid with reports received from radar sites, ground observers, the radio listening service, and the *Fühlungshalter* aircraft that flew alongside the bomber formations giving any changes to their course and looking for gaps in the spacing of the boxes. As the raid progressed, each of the *Jagdkorps* operations rooms charted the raid on large 30ft by 40ft plotting screens and sent directives down to the *Jagddivisionen*, which had tactical command and control of their subordinated formations throughout the battle and were responsible for ensuring the execution of the plan.

The communications moved back and forth as the *Jagddivisionen* kept the *Jagdkorps* apprised of developments and also informed neighboring and subordinate commands at every level. All the organizations used a comprehensive running commentary on the overall air situation broadcast on a common radio frequency, the *Reichsjägerwelle*, which allowed everyone to follow the raid so that an exchange of information on enemy formations could take place.

One of the most useful parts of the German command and control system was their "followers," long-range bombers that picked up the formation and followed, passing information to the controllers as the mission progressed. They did not, as many American aircrew believed, control fighters. (NARA)

By the second half of 1943, each Luftwaffe *Jagddivision* had its own set of warning systems that provided up-to-the-minute information into the *Jagddivision* operations center, which in turn relayed the information to the fighter control battalion. Once the air situation picture was developed, all the available German fighters were launched by the operations center controller and were guided to the formations. The timing of this launch was important, since the single-engine fighters had only about 80 minutes of flying time. Carrying a centerline external fuel tank increased this time but slowed the rate of climb.

Controlling the fighters

The standard day fighter control system was the *Y-Verfahren* (Y-system), called by the Allies "Benito," which had been developed for the German night fighter force. The ground fighter control station consisted of a plotting board and a direction finding (DF) tower, with five radio operation systems, each with an omnidirectional transmitter, an omnidirectional receiver, and a direction finder.

The fighter control station transmitted a signal which was picked up by the "Y-fighter," one of the fighters equipped with a modified German VHF transceiver, the FuG 16ZY, in the fighter formation. This transceiver repeated the signal back to the station, making a type of reverse radio homing. The fighter formation's position was then plotted by the fighter control station on the plotting board and, using the most current information on the bombers' attack route, the fighter control station vectored the Y-fighter's formation towards the bombers' route.

Only one aircraft in the formation activated the FuG 16ZY, and if this aircraft went out of action another predesignated aircraft served as its replacement. Interestingly, the Y-fighter was not the flight leader because, in addition to the ground controller channel, the flight leader had to listen to the common radio frequency broadcasting the *Reichsjägerwelle*'s running commentary on the overall air situation broadcast.

The Y-system made use of capabilities built into the standard FuG 16ZY transceiver, so it became operational very quickly and was generally effective.

Bases and landing fields

The RLV commanders recognized that one of the great problems with the German air defense system was lack of depth, and one of their most useful and innovative solutions was establishing a system of auxiliary airfields designated *Jagdstutzpunkte* (fighter support points). The main ones had ground personnel, fuel, and ammunition stocks to refuel and rearm the fighters so that they could reattack the bomber formations on their return to England, while others were small and only had fuel to allow the fighter to fly to a main *Jagdstutzpunkt*.

All the pilots had maps of these *Jagdstutzpunkte*, and when the RLV

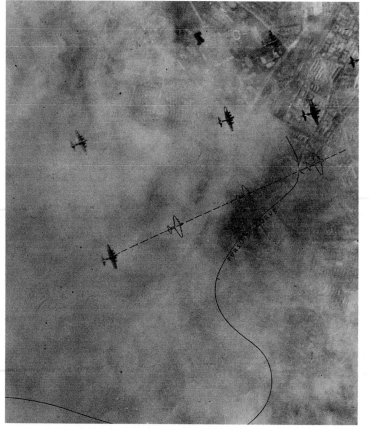

An American intelligence diagram of how a German fighter would make a beam pass, known as a "pursuit curve". This pass was easier for an inexperienced fighter pilot and made for much more accurate shooting for the attacker, but also exposed him to a great deal of defensive fire. (NARA)

fighters ran low on gas and/or ammunition they could land to rearm and refuel at these small alternative airfields and take off to engage the bomber formations again. If there were several similar fighters on the field, after refueling and rearming the highest-ranking pilot became the group leader and, irrespective of the unit to which they belonged, formed them into a single unit for mass attacks controlled by the area *Jagddivision*. This capability to land, refuel/rearm, and attack the returning bomber formations paid huge dividends during the great battles of summer and fall 1943.

Flak

The Germans used antiaircraft guns, or flak, as a point defense, and in each *Jagddivision* controllers had specialist flak liaison officers, a "flak mission commissar" in the control room. There was a need for personal liaison between the commanders of day fighters and flak, and there was a tactical manual that laid down procedures for coordination between day fighters and flak and detailed the exchange of tactical information to avoid confusion and accidents at the border and in the fighter and flak defensive zones.

In action, the flak gunners used radar to find the target's range, even in clear weather, and optics for angle information. They aimed at the lead aircraft in a formation and fired all guns in salvoes. When the radar and optics were not available, this had to be changed to barrage fire to saturate a sector, but constant barrage fire used ammunition at an unsustainable rate.

Germany's best-known flak piece was the 8.8cm Flak 18/36/37, which comprised about 60 percent of Germany's heavy flak guns during World War II. The gun fired a 20.3lb shell to an effective ceiling of 26,000ft.

There was also a 12.8cm gun, the 12.8cm Flak 40, which fired a 57.2lb shell to a maximum ceiling of 35,000ft. These Flak 40s were manned by Germany's best flak gunners and were considered to be the cream of the flak arm.

The numerous, famous, and deadly German 8.8cm antiaircraft gun, which was also an effective antitank weapon. The rings on the barrel indicate hits on aircraft, not necessarily kills. (Bundesarchiv, Bild Bild 1011-635-3999-24, Fotograf: Walther.)

Assessment

The command and control technology may have been new, but it reflected the long-time strengths of the German command and control practices. The Luftwaffe, like all of the German military, operated on the principle of *Auftragstaktik*, a set of simple, commonly accepted and understood operation concepts that provided a common basis for action in the absence of orders. The system, although centralized, was not excessively hierarchical and information was shared widely. Simplified, it meant that commanders were to give their subordinates general directions as to what was to be done and then get of the way and let them get on with it.

Like so much German military innovation, ideas percolated up from below, and after the ideas were scrutinized, if they were recognized as superior practices they were implemented by a senior officer. While the entire command and control system was designed to achieve unity of action through centralization of authority, the actual conduct of combat operations still depended on the initiative of individual commanders.

By 1943 the RAF night bombers used communications-jamming aircraft for every raid, and beginning in July 1943 the RAF started using highly effective *Window* chaff jamming of

A captured B-17 being examined by German pilots. Yellow tape marks the vulnerable spots, notably the large area between the engines that marks the position of the very vulnerable "Tokyo tanks" on late model B-17Fs. (NARA)

German radar. For unknown reasons, during 1943 the Americans generally allowed the early warning radars and fighter communications of the German command and control system to operate almost unhindered, and USAAF bomber formations did not use *Window* until late November 1943. The Americans were also well behind the British in using the *Carpet* radar jammer targeted at the 560MHz German *Würzburg* radar.

A postwar American evaluation of this German command and control system said:

> The information flow … simplified and improved evaluation at all levels, assuring the ultimate formation of the simplest possible air situation picture and speeded up the interchange of basic but relevant intelligence and assured the timely receipt by those actually engaged in combat… The flow of information was [relatively slow] since it was consumed at all levels by the coordination, combination, and evaluation processes [but] produced a greatly simplified and coherent situation picture.

Luftwaffe tactics evolve

The German RLV controllers were innovative and versatile in developing tactics for coordinated fighter attacks against US bomber formations. Aided by the *Fühlungshalter* contact keepers, they watched the formations in order to try to take advantage of any weaknesses if one formation was out of position.

The controllers tried, often but not always successfully, to set up two types of attacks in sequence against a bomber *Pulk*. First, a large formation of rocket-firing fighters was brought in from behind at the same altitude as the *Pulk*. Some single-engine fighters carried two rockets, usually in the ratio of one *Staffel* per *Gruppe*, but the best rocket fighters were the twin-engine fighters which carried four rockets. The rocket fighters made their first attacks from the rear, firing off their 21cm rockets from 1,000m, outside the range of the defensive gunners. The hope was that the rockets might destroy a few bombers and damage others, but their main purpose was to weaken the cohesiveness of the combat boxes.

While the rocket-firing fighters approached the *Pulk*, a larger force of single-engine fighters without rockets flew ahead, parallel to but above and offset from the B-17s. When the rockets exploded in the formation and scattered it, the formation of single-engine fighters would perform a 180-degree turn and make a mass head-on attack from in a dive, the famous "12 o'Clock High" attack. The RLV pilots perfected their head-on attacks by making practice attacks on Junkers Ju 88s flying at 23,000ft at the B-17's cruising speed, and found that attacks from 10 degrees above and dead ahead were the best. Column attacks worked best since they removed the chance of two aircraft colliding as they attacked the same bomber. At first, the fighter units made the attacks in two columns, but they found that the columns got in each other's way, so they moved to single columns. After the attack, in theory, the formation would reform and attack another B-17 *Pulk*, but often the German formation was itself split up and single German fighters would attack and try to shoot down single B-17s that had dropped out of the formation.

This was a major problem. Galland realized that the bomber formations had to be attacked by fighter formations and broken up first, and as the campaign developed in the fall, he issued tactical orders on how to attack the bomber force; but the situation got so bad that in the early fall, fighter unit commanders were ordered to fly missions as "flying commissars" to observe the degree of determination with which their units attacked and make sure they continued their mass attacks and did not split off to attack crippled bombers.

Captured US aircraft

The Germans had a number of captured US aircraft, and in 1943 they formed a group of these aircraft that served to familiarize German fighter pilots with the strengths and weaknesses of their opponents' aircraft. This unit, the 2nd Staffel of the Versuchtverband Oberkommando der Luftwaffe (the Trials and Research Unit of the Luftwaffe High Command, or Ob.d.L.), first tested and flew the captured aircraft. Once they had been thoroughly flown and tested, they were flown in a group to different front-line units, a collection known eponymously as the Wanderzirkus Rosarius (Rosarius' travelling circus).

A B-17 was of special interest to the Luftwaffe's fighter pilots, and diagrams from the tests showed the defensive guns' locations and firing arcs and, more importantly, where the fuel tanks were located. One German pilot noted that he knew exactly how fast the top turret could turn.

Air-to-air combat

Once the Americans began to fly bombing missions into Germany that could be escorted part of the way, the RLV controllers tried to keep their fighters away from the formations until the American escorts ran low on fuel and had to leave the bombers. At that point the controller sent the German fighters to attack the bombers. One disadvantage of this procedure was that once the P-47 pilots realized they would not be attacked on the way to the rendezvous with the bombers, they developed techniques for extending the range of their fighters, notably climbing at a very slow rate at a fuel-saving power setting, and thus were able to increase their range.

The result of the controllers keeping the RLV fighters away from the escorts was that for much of the American daylight bombing campaign in 1943 there was relatively little air-to-air combat between German single-seat fighters and American P-47 escorts. As the P-47s extended their range in late July, they were occasionally able to engage the twin-engine *Zerstörer* laden with rockets and cannon or the twin-engine German night fighters, and these were easy targets.

When the P-47s engaged the German single-engine fighters, the contest was much more equal. At lower altitude the German fighters were more than a match for the P-47, and Thunderbolt pilots were advised to avoid combats at low altitudes and slow speeds. The P-47's performance progressively improved above 15,000ft, and between 20,000ft and 30,000ft, where many of the engagements began, it was superior to the single-engine German fighters except for rate of climb and acceleration. However, overall when a dogfight began on relatively equal terms the outcome was determined by pilot skill.

CAMPAIGN OBJECTIVES
Prelude to D-Day

A very late-model B-17F with a chin nose turret. This turret was developed for the unsuccessful YB-40; it proved very effective and some were mounted on late-model B-17Fs. It was standard equipment on the B-17G which began to arrive in theater in September 1943 and the turret was very popular because it gave the bombardier more space to operate. The turret made the B-17G slightly slower than the B-17F and this, combined with the greater space for the bombardier, made it the B-17 of choice for lead aircrews. (NARA)

The objectives for the American Eighth Air Force were outlined in the CBO directive of May 18, 1943: to defeat the Luftwaffe's day fighter force both by bombing aircraft production facilities and by destroying the day fighter force in air combat, in order to allow the invasion of Europe from England. The operation was given the name *Pointblank*. As previously noted, the CCS made it clear that the objective of *Pointblank* was not to win the war – the ground forces of the Allies would do that. *Pointblank*'s aim was to make the invasion possible.

There was another unspoken but almost equally important objective for the USAAF leaders, who were virtually all the product of the prewar Air Corps Tactical School, and that was to prove that an independently operating strategic air force could do what no navy or ground forces could, namely destroy an enemy's war material production capability with pinpoint daylight strategic bombing. This, the USAAF leaders thought, would allow the formation of an independent US Air Force after the war, just as the RAF had been founded in April 1918 specifically to carry out strategic bombing against Germany.

The USAAF won its first battle when the Eighth Air Force commander, General Ira Eaker, was able to convince Winston Churchill and the Combined Chiefs of Staff to allow Eighth Air Force to carry out a daylight strategic bombing campaign. Despite having much of its equipment diverted in late 1942 to Operation *Torch*, Eaker's VIII Bomber Command slowly but steadily built up its bomber forces and began to fly missions into Germany.

General Eaker seemed to feel he was doing missionary work with his initially small force of bombers, but he believed it would affect the whole future of day bombardment in this war – and thus the formation of an independent air force after the war. He carefully followed the Air Corps Tactical School doctrine and operated under the assumption that its unescorted bomber formations would be able to carry out their strikes without unacceptable losses, usually given as 10 percent. The bombers developed formations that gave the maximum firepower while developments such as "lead crews" made their bombing effective.

Army Air Force headquarters fully appreciated the critical character of the experiment being carried out by the Eighth Air Force, and its leaders were anxious for Eaker to prove the validity of their daylight bombing theories. The result was that Eaker forwarded every mission report that could be interpreted as an air victory, or as a demonstration of the USAAF doctrine of strategic bombardment, to Washington. Eaker and the leadership especially promoted the honest but wildly exaggerated German fighter kill claims by the bombers' gunners because bad weather over Germany meant that the bombing of German war material production was only marginally effective.

VIII Bomber Command received a steady flow of bomber replacements, but this was offset by a similar flow of replacements the Germans were receiving and the ever-increasing losses the Germans were able to inflict, endangering the main campaign objective.

VIII Fighter Command P-47s were able to accompany the bombers only as far as the German–Belgian border because of the failure to develop reliable external fuel tanks and the larger failure to develop a long-range escort fighter. More escort fighters arrived but General Eaker did not give priority to the development and deployment of external fuel tanks, so even the increase in escort fighters could not cut bomber losses.

Because Eighth Air Force did not change its main weapons, the B-17 bomber and P-47 escort, and because its mission to destroy the German day fighter force stayed the same, VIII Bomber Command could not change tactics during the campaign, relying on numbers to reach the target. The campaign resulted in heavy losses for the bombers, but because of the continuing wildly exaggerated claims by the bombers' gunners, General Eaker and to a lesser extent General Arnold, chief of the Army Air Forces, believed that they were fulfilling the primary campaign objective of destroying the Luftwaffe day fighter force. In fact, the Luftwaffe fighter force was stronger at the end of 1943 than when the campaign began.

THE CAMPAIGN

Flying against the factories

The Eighth's first campaigns

A Wfr. Gr. 21 passing under a B-17, probably in the summer of 1943 since the distinctive tail fin markings have not been applied. (NARA)

VIII Bomber Command began its daylight strategic bombing campaign modestly on August 17, 1942 with a raid on Rouen-Sotteville in France by 12 B-17s. At that point Eighth Air Force consisted of three bomb groups and four fighter groups, two flying Spitfires and two flying P-38s.

On October 9, 1942, VIII Bomber Command flew its first truly large-scale mission to Lille in France with 108 heavy bombers, including two dozen Consolidated B-24 Liberators on their first mission. The Luftwaffe made its first real effort against the American bombers, easily slipped past the large escort of British and American fighters, and shot down three B-17 and one B-24, as well as damaging many more.

On this mission a problem arose that was to haunt VIII Bomber Command right through to the end of 1943. The bombers' gunners claimed 56 German fighters destroyed and 26 probables, an impossible score since it would have accounted for 15 percent of the estimated Luftwaffe fighter strength in western Europe. However, since Eighth Air Force's primary campaign objective was to destroy the Luftwaffe's day fighter arm, these claims went unchallenged. In fact, the Germans lost one fighter that day.

But the attack on Lille was to be followed by a pause in the Eighth's campaign. The Allies had decided that there would be no invasion of mainland Europe in the near future, and instead prepared to invade North Africa with Operation *Torch*. The commander of the USAAF, General Henry "Hap" Arnold, and the USAAF planners did not find it easy to reconcile *Torch* with their original conception of a combined bomber offensive from the United Kingdom. VIII Bomber Command's mission of preparing for an invasion of Europe would have to be postponed indefinitely. The USAAF leaders accepted the plan only after a vigorous dissent, and for the remainder of 1942 they continued to consider *Torch* a diversion from the objective of destroying the Luftwaffe and the Germans' war production capability.

Eighth Air Force soon lost much of its strength to the Mediterranean theater as General Arnold had to order the transfer of two B-24 groups plus four P-38 fighter groups to North Africa, followed by two B-17 groups and nearly all the rest of the P-38s, leaving Eighth Air Force with no fighters in England. The Eighth also lost its commander, and General Eaker took his place.

The movements left VIII Fighter Command with only two squadrons of Spitfires, though P-47s were expected in March. The remaining bombers mainly attacked submarine pens with a heavy RAF Spitfire escort, but on November 23 the Germans made a drastic change in tactics when a *Gruppenkommandeur* (group commander), Hauptmann Egon Mayer, led the first head-on attack on a formation of 36 B-17s attacking St Nazaire, shooting down four and seriously damaging another. It was so successful that the rest of the Luftwaffe single-engine day fighter force adapted it as standard.

VIII Bomber Command's first raid into Germany was on January 27, 1943, when 55 B-17s flew a four-hour unescorted mission to the port city of Wilhelmshaven, losing three bombers. In February, most VIII Bomber Command missions were against submarine pens and support facilities.

Following the November 1942 invasion of North Africa, in March 1943 two B-24 groups returned from Africa. Both groups were understrength, but on March 18 the two Liberator groups flew their first mission. Because they were faster than the B-17s, the B-24 groups had to keep their own formation within the larger bomber stream and did not benefit from the mutual support of the B-17 groups. With only two groups of Liberators, and with more and more B-17 groups arriving in England every month, General Eaker began assigning the B-24s to tasks other than daylight bombing, though some continued to join the B-17 missions.

At the end of March both B-24 groups were relieved from combat operations altogether to train for a classified mission: a low-level attack on the Romanian oil fields at Ploesti. Another recently returned B-24 group joined them when it arrived in England, and all three groups then left for North Africa and temporary duty with the Ninth Air Force, though another soon arrived.

Heavily armed German night fighters often attacked damaged stragglers. Here a German Bf 110G night fighter pulls off an attack on a B-17. The light gray night fighters had one wing painted black so if they were caught in a searchlight the German flak would not fire on them. (NARA)

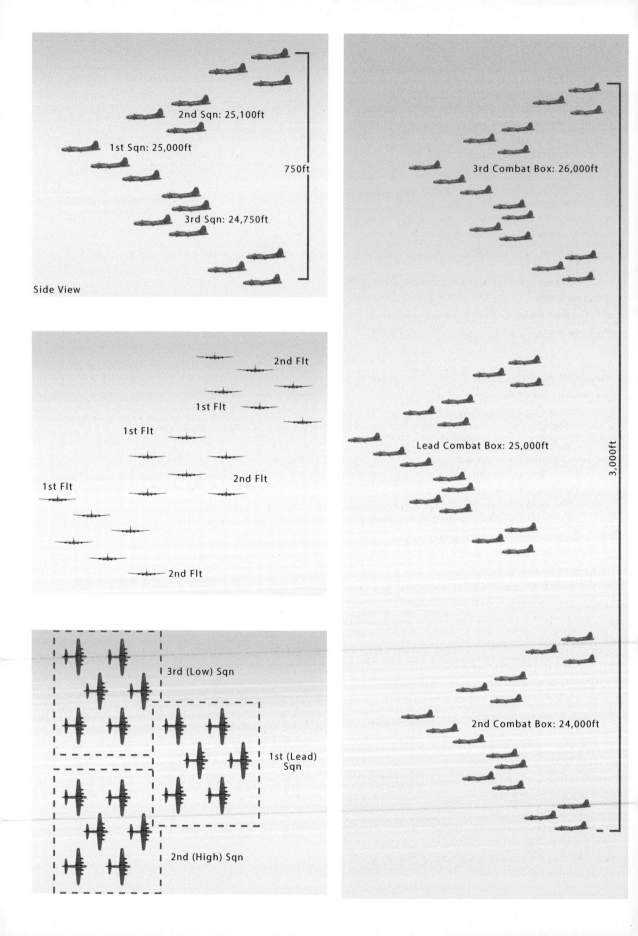

Side View

2nd Sqn: 25,100ft

1st Sqn: 25,000ft

750ft

3rd Sqn: 24,750ft

2nd Flt

1st Flt

1st Flt

1st Flt

2nd Flt

2nd Flt

3rd (Low) Sqn

1st (Lead) Sqn

2nd (High) Sqn

3rd Combat Box: 26,000ft

Lead Combat Box: 25,000ft

3,000ft

2nd Combat Box: 24,000ft

OPPOSITE: B-17 FORMATIONS, 1943

From late 1942 when the Luftwaffe began to aggressively attack, the primary concern of VIII Bomber Command's formations was defensive. The first step was to have the bombers bomb in formation and drop when a "lead crew" dropped, rather than each bomber dropping on its own. For formations, VIII Bomber Command first tried 18-aircraft formations in column in early 1943, but it soon became obvious that they would have to concentrate their formations to provide more firepower. To this end, rather than sending bombers in columns, VII Bomber Command decided in late April 1943 to stack the wing's groups, one 18-ship formation above and one below the lead group, and the other combat wings would follow three miles behind. The large formations had many disadvantages – the major one being that they were very hard to maneuver with course changes – but they were still the most effective formation in terms of defensive firepower. Another disadvantage was that the extremities of the formations were very vulnerable since they lacked support from the rest of the group. The lower corner of the low squadron – the easiest for the German fighters to reach – was the most vulnerable, and was referred to as "Purple Heart Corner."

A third disadvantage was that the high group often lost sight of the lead group if the lead group turned, and the formation spread out – a sure invitation for a German attack. The formations were constantly "tweaked" to try to improve their defensive capabilities, but there really was no perfect formation developed. In any of these formations, if a bomber was hit and dropped out of formation, it was usually quickly set upon and shot down.

On April 26, 1943, 115 B-17s were sent to bomb the Focke-Wulf factory at Bremen. This was the largest force sent by VIII Bomber Command to a single target and the 1st Bombardment Wing tried a new combat wing formation, three 18-plane boxes "vertically stacked." The second box flew above and behind the lead box, and the third box below and behind the leader. The 54 aircraft made a formation 600 yards long, over a mile wide, and half a mile deep. On this mission there were two combat wings in trail.

The force flew across the North Sea out of the range of the best of the German coastal fighter squadrons, but the German controllers, advised of the bombers' course by their "shadowers," kept their fighters on the alert until the shadowers reported that the bombers were crossing the German coast and had a 5-mile gap between the first and second combat wings; at which point the German fighters exploited the gap as they began their head-on attacks. The B-17s flying in the least well-protected parts of their formations – on the edges of the combat boxes or lagging behind – were the first to be attacked. Sixteen B-17s were shot down, all from the three combat boxes of the leading combat wing, in part because the German fighters had plenty of room in front of the lead formation to line up their attacks. As was always to be the case, damaged bombers that dropped out of formation left holes in the combat boxes, which increased the vulnerability of the remaining aircraft. They also made tempting targets, and three kills of these cripples were credited to long-range Bf 110G night fighters which caught withdrawing bombers.

Despite these losses, the bombing was accurate and the Focke-Wulf factory was severely damaged, temporarily losing 50 percent of its capacity. But this success came at the highest cost to date, 14 percent of the force, when a 10 percent loss rate was considered the maximum VIII Bomber Command could accept on a sustained basis.

The combat report blamed the losses on the 5-mile gap between the first and second wings, which prevented mutual support, but the tightness of the formation was also an issue. The leading wing was in a looser formation, which made attacking it a more attractive prospect than the second wing, which flew in closer formation, forming a "vertical wall" that discouraged head-on attacks. The second wing had no losses, and even with the first wing's losses – blamed on their loose formation – the defensive effectiveness of the 54-bomber combat wing seemed clear, and it became the standard formation used by the Eighth Air Force.

An Fw 190 makes a diving break-off after a head-on attack on a B-17 formation. Based on the range, the German fighter had probably made his attack on the formation ahead of the one in the picture. (NARA)

Escorts

By March three fighter groups were equipped with P-47s but had not been used as bomber escorts because of extensive engine problems and especially radio problems. General Frank Hunter, commander of VIII Fighter Command, initially used them mainly for fighter sweeps; however, in May he finally, after prodding from USAAF headquarters, began to employ them to escort the bombers. For the escort mission the P-47's major limitation was range. At this point it was not fitted with any sort of external fuel tank and it only had a combat radius of action of less than 200 miles.

Reinforcements and increasing range

In May 1943 Eighth Air Force received six new bombardment groups, five of them with new model B-17Fs equipped with long-range "Tokyo" tanks. The reinforcements allowed the formation of a new bomb wing, the 4th Bomb Wing, with three groups, and the new groups meant that VIII Bomber Command now had the potential to send over 200 bombers a day to a target. The increased range of the new B-17s was very important to mission planners because, as much as possible, the bomber formations did not want to fly a straight-line route to the target. The aim was to conceal the ultimate target from the German controllers for as long as possible, and the longer-range B-17s allowed more and longer feints. German single-seat fighters could stay airborne for about 80 minutes with their external 80-gallon fuel tanks, and it was hoped that if the bomber force made in-flight route changes this would lead the German controllers to send fighters in the wrong direction and they would have less time to engage the bombers when they finally found the formations.

On May 14, 1943, VIII Bomber Command launched a record bomber force of 236 aircraft to attack Kiel, 460 miles away from England and the longest mission yet attempted. The main force was B-17s accompanied by one severely understrength group of B-24s; the single B-24 group drew the heaviest enemy attacks and lost five of their eight aircraft, at least partly because the performance characteristics of the B-24s prevented them from staying close enough to the Fortresses for protection. It was clear that the different flight characteristics made it practically impossible to fly B-17 and B-24 units together in a single formation. The B-24 groups had to be in a separate formation large enough to take care of themselves, and this made them almost useless for deep-penetration missions.

On May 21, VIII Bomber Command sent nine B-17 groups from the two wings deep into Germany, well beyond P-47 range, for the first time. The 1st Wing went to Wilhelmshaven while the 4th Wing attacked Emden. At both targets the German fighter controller used large numbers of fighters to attack the leading elements of the bomber formations with head-on passes during the target run, indicating to the Americans that the Germans understood the "lead bomber" technique that had been in use since early 1943. The result was that bombing was erratic, and some targets were completely missed, but losses were modest – five B-17s from the 4th Wing and seven from the 1st Wing.

However, the most important development of the May 21 missions was the intervention of the German weapons test unit, Erprobungskommando 25, which for the first time used the Wfr. Gr. 21 air-to-air rocket, reported by the bomber crews as "flaming baseballs."

Though the Americans reported no losses to the weapons, one of the German test pilots claimed a B-17 with his Wfr. Gr. 21, the first victory claimed for this powerful rocket, which later in 1943 would become the weapon of choice for breaking up the bomber *Pulks*. The rockets and launchers were sent to two fighter units, but they were not popular because they hindered the fighters' maneuverability.

An American intelligence diagram showing how a German fighter would break down and away after a head-on pass. (NARA)

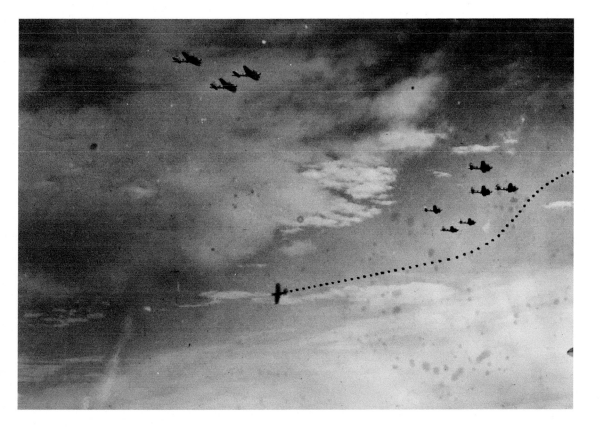

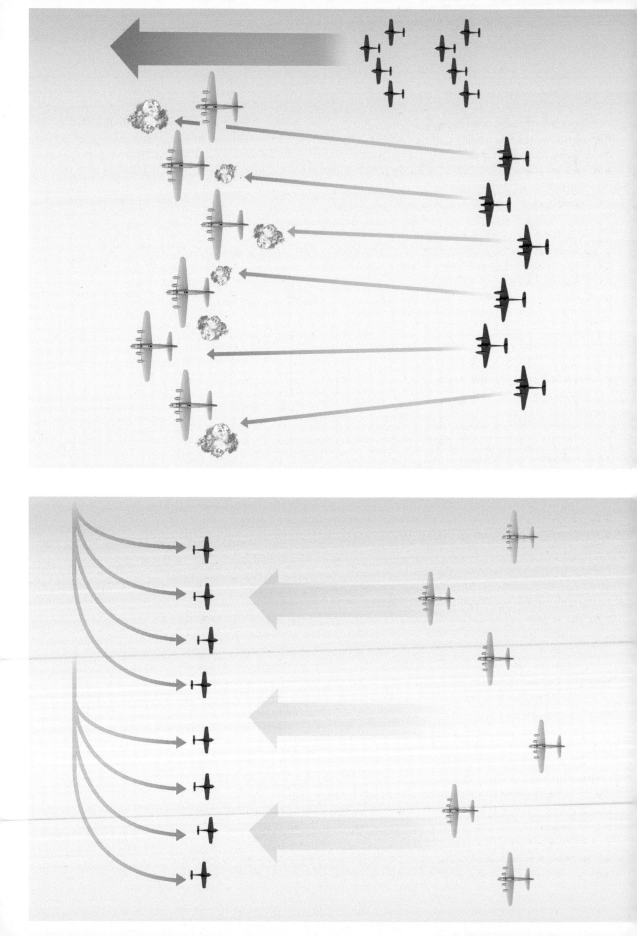

OPPOSITE: FIGHTER MASS ATTACK

In the fall of 1943, the Germans began to equip their Bf 110 and Me 410 *Zerstörers* with the Wfr. Gr. 21 aerial rocket to break up the American bomber formations, and with the development and deployment of these weapons the Luftwaffe developed a method of coordinating the firepower of the rocket-armed fighters with their classic head-on "12 o'Clock High" attack. A formation of *Zerstörers* would be joined by a formation of single-seat fighters that would position themselves above and fly parallel to the *Zerstörers*. As the *Zerstörers* approached the bomber formation from behind, the single-seat fighter formation would accelerate and climb to get in front of the bomber formation. Once they were well in front of the bomber formation, they turned toward the bombers and the *Zerstörers* would fire their rockets into the formation. The Wfr. Gr. 21 explosions would make the bomber formations spread out and make it much less dangerous for the single-engine fighters to attack.

As the single-engine fighters climbed above the bomber formations they slowed down, and when they rolled in for the attack, they tried to attack from a ten-degree dive. By slowing in the climb before they rolled in, the fighters gave themselves a little more time to line up on the targets, but when they reached the bombers from their dive the combined closing speed was about 500mph. The fighters often attacked in a staggered formation to reduce the danger of a collision if both were attacking the same bomber.

On May 29, VIII Bomber Command dispatched a record 279 bombers, the 1st Wing to St Nazaire and La Pallice and the 4th Wing to the Rennes marshalling yard. This mission was the debut of the YB-40s, B-17s converted to heavy escort fighters, and seven were sent out with leading elements of the 1st Wing to St Nazaire. When the escort turned back, the Germans attacked for two hours, some of the RLV pilots flying two sorties; 16 B-17s were lost and the YB-40s were of little help. Additionally, after the B-17s dropped their bombs, the YB-40s, still laden with ammunition, could not keep pace and forced the whole formation to reduce speed.

The Combined Bomber Offensive

The Combined Bomber Offensive officially began on June 10, 1943, and the next day seven bomb groups from the 1st Bomb Wing and three from the 4th were sent to bomb Bremen. Weather forced the entire force to divert to targets of opportunity where conditions were better, but this scattered the formations and they lost mutual support. German controllers launched a total of 218 sorties and eight B-17s were lost, seven from the leading combat wing; the brunt of these attacks hit the newly formed groups flying the high-group position. Six of these losses were from one of the newly arrived groups, which had now lost nine B-17s, about a quarter of the group, in its first two missions.

The Luftwaffe was using the Wfr. Gr. 21 rockets to break up the *Pulks*, and for this mission tried another new weapon, the RZ 65 rocket. Several Bf 109F fighters from Erprobungskommando (ErprKdo) 25 intercepted the force with these rockets carried in a streamlined container that produced very little drag, but the rocket was too small to be effective. Two weeks later two RZ 65-equipped Bf 109Fs tried again, led by the commander of ErprKdo 25, but his report was sufficiently pessimistic that further trials were canceled.

The P-47s had begun to escort the bombers, but in June the Assistant Secretary of War for Air, Robert A. Lovett, visited VIII Fighter Command to discuss the problem of escort fighters. Lovett expressed Arnold's concern that the P-47s were not being used for escort, and after the visit General Frank Hunter, Eighth Air Force Fighter Command commander, told Eaker that he was afraid that Lovett wanted the longer-range P-38s brought to the theater. Hunter thought the P-47 was better, but this showed his fundamental misunderstanding of the air battle over Germany. The issue was how to get longer-range fighters to break up the mass head-on attacks as well as the rocket-firing fighters' attacks from the rear. After Lovett's

A B-17 going down with fire in its Tokyo tanks while still under attack by an Fw 190. The Fw 190 was violating orders by attacking a single B-17 instead of trying to break up the formation. (NARA)

visit, on June 26 Arnold sent Eaker a cable expressing "grave concern of your employment of fighters… [you are getting] meager results with our best high altitude escort fighter."

On June 13, the 1st and 4th Wings were sent to Bremen, but clouds caused the diversion of most bombers to Kiel and targets of opportunity. The two wings came from different directions, and the 1st Bomb Wing saw little opposition and lost only four B-17s, though its bombing was poor.

Things were very different for the 4th Wing. Their four boxes were led by a new commander using an experimental formation that he had devised, but this proved a disaster. The 4th was under heavy attack from the coast to the targets and the design prevented many bombers from firing directly ahead, the preferred direction of the German attacks. One group lost seven B-17s before they reached the target, including the one flown by the new commander who had designed the formation.

To make things even worse, as one of 4th Wing's groups returned over the North Sea some gunners assumed that the danger from the Luftwaffe had passed and began to strip and clean their machine guns, but just off the English coast German night fighters appeared and quickly shot down several B-17s.

Overall, the 4th Wing lost 22 B-17s on the mission, which marked the wing's first month of combat. Prior to this mission the month had been a hard one – 20 bombers and over 200 airmen had been lost on the wing's eight unescorted missions – and now the 22 lost on this mission added to the problem. One of the 4th Wing groups had lost nearly half the original crews and aircraft after only nine missions.

It was becoming clear that the 4th Wing's B-17Fs with their "Tokyo tanks" were especially vulnerable to German fire, but there was nothing to be done. They could not be removed in the field, and even if they could have been their extra range was more important than their increased vulnerability.

On June 22, VIII Bomber Command flew the first mission under the new CBO target list, an attack on the synthetic rubber plant at Hüls, which produced 30 percent of Germany's total output. Of the 230 Fortresses on the raid, 182 attacked Hüls, with the remaining 48 attacking the chemical plants, and the two wings were accompanied by 11 YB-40s, including five in the leading combat box where the major attacks were expected. German attacks were directed against the leading group where the YB-40s were, but the group lost five aircraft and the YB-40s' defensive contribution seemed negligible.

However, this was VIII Bomber Command's most effective strategic strike so far. The bombing was extremely accurate – one quarter of the bombs exploded within the factory area; it rendered the plant totally inoperative for a month, and full production was not resumed for six months. German reports noted later that a follow-up raid could have stopped its rubber production entirely, but at this early stage of the bombing campaign the American planners did not understand that major targets had to be hit several times to achieve their destruction, even if the first raids were effective. A second raid never came, and the synthetic rubber industry, a true choke point in the German war machine, escaped and was diversified.

Weather continued to be a major problem; for the rest of June and early July bad weather covered the continent and the bombers achieved little in the way of striking the CBO targets. On a June 25 raid against Hamburg, the weather disrupted the bomber stream so badly that some formations were scattered among the towering banks of cloud and the separated groups had to either pick out targets of opportunity or bring their bombs home. The weather was also a problem for German fighters, which had to take off and land in it, and bad weather made it harder to find the American bombers once airborne, but when they did find the scattered formations they scored well, shooting down 18 B-17s. The bombers' gunners claimed 62 victories but the Germans lost only 15 fighters, most to weather-related accidents.

However, VIII Bomber Command was able to score some successes against CBO targets, even on short-range escorted missions. On July 14 it bombed a number of airfields in France and at one, Villacoublay, it destroyed an Fw 190 repair facility and 70 Fw 190s. On June 26, the B-17s returned to Villacoublay, where losses were light but the Germans surprised a group of P-47s and shot down five.

New markings

In July VIII Bomber Command gave a significant if unintended morale boost to its bomber units. At the beginning of VIII Bomber Command's operations, the only way an aircraft's squadron could be identified was by the letters on the side, but in early July Eighth Air Force introduced a much more visible means of group identification. Each B-17 bombardment wing was given a white symbol containing a blue letter to be displayed on the tail fins. Fortresses of the 1st Bombardment Wing had a triangle symbol, those of the 4th Wing a square, and a different letter within these symbols identified the particular group. The change was very popular and from that point on the group members identified themselves by this sign, e.g. "I'm in the Triangle A" (91st Bomb Group) or "I'm in the Square D" (100th Bomb Group), etc.

The midsummer situation

During the summer VIII Bomber Command expanded in size to 16 groups of B-17s and four of B-24s, and now there were 580 B-17s, of which approximately 400 could be counted on to be airworthy for any one mission.

A B-17 crew strapping on their parachutes prior to take-off. From the number of nose guns this picture was probably taken in mid-1943. (NARA)

With the terrible weather in June and early July, VIII Bomber Command leaders began to wonder if there would ever be a settled period of weather to permit a major strike at the CBO priority targets in Germany. Finally, towards the end of July 1943, RAF meteorologists reported that the virtually continuous weather "lows" that had been passing over northwest Europe for the better part of three months would finally be giving way to a clear weather high. Based on this perhaps optimistic forecast and under considerable pressure from General Arnold, VIII Bomber Command began a series of sustained attacks in a massive attempt to begin to meet the objectives of the CBO. From July 25–30 VIII Bomber Command flew large missions almost every day in what the Command dubbed the "Fortress Blitz."

Facing off

For both the Eighth Air Force and the Luftwaffe the mode of battle had changed little, and each side was aware of the tactics and devices the other would be likely to employ, though both were apprehensive of some new device or technique. Planners at Eighth Bomber

Command strove to outwit the enemy's fighter defenses by feints, diversions, and divided missions timed to play upon the limited flight duration of enemy fighters, and often the number of losses hinged upon how well these plans worked.

On the German side, defense controllers were not easily fooled and were able to deploy strong fighter opposition against every mission. The repetitious Luftwaffe tactic of frontal assault against the leading bomber boxes, usually during the crucial period of the bomb run, remained very effective, and the Fortress squadron flying the low group in the leading wing of a deep penetration mission – known as "Purple Heart Corner" – knew they would be in for a very difficult mission.

Unfortunately, the Americans still tended to overestimate the effectiveness of their defending gunfire and believed that the German fighter force was being decimated by the Eighth's bombers' gunners, which gave them the very skewed impression that the Luftwaffe day fighter force was being devastated. This was the general impression of the public in Britain and the United States, and to a certain degree also the belief of the commanders, but in July the RLV was to show how far off these estimates were.

A B-17 formation flying through flak on its bomb run – note the open bomb bay doors. Two B-17s in the formation ahead have been hit and will probably become easy prey for German fighters. (NARA)

The battles begin

In late July and early August 1943, the RAF raided Hamburg, marking the first use of *Window* radar jamming chaff, which severally handicapped the German radar. On July 25, VIII Bomber

The first American bomber hit by a Wfr. Gr. 21 was on *The Sack*, but the bomber survived. The hit was unusual because the Wfr. Gr. 21 was very inaccurate. (NARA)

Command joined in the operation. Part of the 1st Bomb Wing attacked Hamburg and Kiel, while the 4th Bomb Wing attacked the Fw 190 works at Warnemunde beyond Kiel, the furthest target yet for VIII Bomber Command. The 1st Wing groups had trouble forming up, resulting in a long, strung-out formation, and when it arrived it found that RAF firebombing the night before had left a 15,000ft pall of smoke over Hamburg that hindered their bombing. Nineteen B-17s were lost, seven of these from the low group, the leading 1st Wing's "Purple Heart Corner," and some of the losses were to Hamburg's vicious flak, which damaged several B-17s that were forced to drop out of formation and were easily picked off.

The next day, July 26, VIII Bomber Command launched 300 bombers and, while the weather was bad over one target, the Hamburg U-boat factories, 92 other B-17s successfully attacked the Continental Gummi Werke at Hanover, a synthetic rubber plant and major tire factory. Although some groups attacked from the unusually high altitude of 31,000ft, the bombing was exceptional and scored 21 direct hits on buildings. Fires and explosions produced a huge column of smoke that rose to 22,000ft, and the resulting damage ended all production for the next three months. Over both targets the RLV fighters concentrated their attacks on the leading Fortress formations. Many fighters flew two missions, and the overall cost to the Americans was 24 bombers.

On July 27 the weather was too bad for VIII Bomber Command missions, but that night almost 800 RAF bombers struck and the combination of warm dry weather and damage to Hamburg's firefighting equipment from the previous raids contributed to an enormous firestorm that devastated the city. The raids killed over 40,000 people, causing great fear in the Nazi leadership that if four or five more German cities were destroyed in the same fashion the regime would collapse.

The day everything changed

On July 28 the weather was still marginal, but VIII Bomber Command launched its most ambitious attack yet in support of the CBO objectives, targeting several aircraft factories producing Fw 190s. Altogether, 302 of the heavy bombers were dispatched in two forces, but adverse weather prevented the majority from completing the mission.

The 1st Wing sent 82 B-17s to attack the Fieseler components works at Kassel while the 4th Wing's longer-range B-17s made the deepest penetration into Germany so far, to an Fw 190 assembly plant at Oschersleben. The German controllers tracked the formations and were able to vector over 350 RLV fighters to continuous attacks on both bomber streams, both inbound and on withdrawal, and every day-fighter unit in the area made contact.

On the way to Kassel the 1st Wing was attacked by Bf 109Gs and Fw 190s of both JG 1 and JG 11 firing Wfr. Gr. 21s to break up the formations. No B-17s were shot down but one, *The Sack*, was struck below the top turret by a large fragment that exploded its oxygen bottles and blasted quite an impressive hole.

The 120 B-17s of the 4th Wing hit bad weather and the RLV's attackers included the new Bf 109G-6/U4 with a 30mm MK 108 engine-mounted cannon. Despite the poor weather, the undercast parted just long enough to allow the lead bombardier of one group to recognize a crossroads a few miles from his aiming point. Quickly calculating the time from target, he estimated his release point and 14 others dropped by this signal, while 13 in the group following were also able to make a successful strike. Photo reconnaissance next day revealed an excellent concentration of bombs on the plant.

For the Americans, this day had a breakthrough technical development. Over 1,100 200-gallon droppable paper ferry tanks had been shipped to the United Kingdom, but because of the paper tank's limitations the units were hesitant to use them. On July 28 the 4th Fighter Group attached them to their P-47s, and despite many malfunctions with feeding, the tanks enabled them to pick up the returning B-17s at Emmerich, on the Dutch–German border. The P-47s' surprise appearance broke up what was beginning to be a well-organized attack on the withdrawing 1st Bomb Wing; the P-47s quickly shot down two Fw 190s and four Bf 109s with one P-47 loss, but total US bomber losses were high – 22 B-17s.

The final attack of the week-long "Fortress Blitz" was July 30, when both B-17 wings attacked the Kassel Fw 190 factories, but after the losses and battle damage of the past few days VIII Bomber Command could only muster 186 Fortresses between the two wings. The wings changed tactics and flew in a single, long formation for mutual self-defense and to assist the escorts, but this was offset by the ease with which the German controllers located the entire force soon enough to concentrate fighters to intercept them. The German fighters flew 285 defensive sorties, including 40 second sorties, and the controllers concentrated the defending fighters along the bombers' return route and planned a maximum-strength attack.

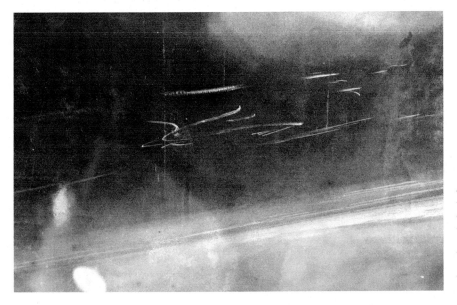

German fighter controllers tried to keep their fighters away from the escorts, but at times it was not possible. These are contrails from a dogfight between German fighters and American escorts. (NARA)

Fortunately for the Americans, all three American P-47 groups – 107 P-47s – were assigned to withdrawal escort and all the Thunderbolts now had the 200-gallon paper drop tanks, so they could fly further in than ever before to meet the returning American bombers. When they arrived they found the bombers under attack by the RLV fighters, and the result was the largest battle to date between American and German fighters. For the loss of seven Thunderbolts, the P-47s shot down 27 RLV fighters. Seventeen B-17s were shot down but the extended range of the Thunderbolts was suddenly a real new concern to the RLV.

Even though the weather was good on the last day of July, the heavy losses of the previous few days left VIII Bomber Command crews exhausted and unable to fly a mission that day.

The "Fortress Blitz" week had been the most strenuous period of operations VIII Bomber Command had experienced in the war. Fifteen B-17 groups with about 330 aircraft and crews began the raids, and by the end of the week nearly half of the bombers participating had sustained some form of damage and about 100 B-17s had been lost or scrapped. Nine hundred aircrew were casualties and were either missing, killed, or wounded, and while aircraft losses were relatively easy to replace, the trained crews were not.

German buildup

A B-17 landing after firing a flare that gave it priority in the traffic pattern, as it alerted the medics to the fact that there were wounded on board the aircraft. The pilot would have already called ahead to have the ambulance waiting. (NARA)

As the American and British raids increased, Hitler criticized Göring more and more. Erhard Milch, effectively second-in-command of the Luftwaffe but more importantly also Chief of Air Armament (Generalluftzeugmeister), and General Adolf Galland, the commander of the German fighter force, (General der Jagdflieger), wanted "absolute emphasis" placed on the air defense of the Reich. Both were far more worried about the growing day offensive which could accurately destroy German industrial choke points than they were about the RAF raids that were devastating German cities but had little effect on the regime's warfare capability.

Hitler's outbursts gave Galland and Milch the opportunity they had been looking for to strengthen the day forces, which came in three ways – formation of new units, expanding existing RLV units, and transferring units from other theaters. Galland had already begun the expansion of the existing RLV day-fighter units. He wanted first to increase the number of *Staffel* in each *Gruppe* from three to four, and then to raise the number of fighters in each *Staffel* from 12 to 16. The total establishment strength of a *Jagdgeschwader* would thus be increased from 124 to 208 fighters.

Reinforcement of the RLV with *Jagdgruppen* (fighter groups) from the Eastern and Southern fronts was also underway and three *Zerstörergruppen* ("destroyer" groups) were recalled from the Eastern and Mediterranean fronts and re-formed into RLV heavy fighter units. Since many of the *Zerstörer* units had been utilized for ground attack, the crews had to be retrained for air-to-air combat, but the heavy armament and long range of the *Zerstörer* vastly enhanced the capabilities of the RLV. Bf 110s and Me 410s could all carry four Wfr. Gr. 21 rocket tubes, and a bewildering variety of subtypes were produced with various combinations of 20mm and 30mm cannon.

Hitler's favorite Me 410 weapon was the BK 5 50mm cannon, developed from an army antitank gun. The cannon equipped one entire Me 410 *Gruppe* but the recoil and feed mechanisms were not designed for the g-forces of aerial combat, so they could rarely get off more than one shot without jamming.

Milch also began to plan for a significant increase in the production of the Bf 109, Fw 190, and Me 410 day fighters, which were the only types immediately available, and he and Speer's accomplishments were amazing. In 1943 the German factories and repair facilities produced 11,241 single-seat fighters and 2,613 twin-engine fighters, and the Luftwaffe fighter strength rose from 1,348 at the end of 1942 to over 2,000 at the beginning of October 1943. Additionally, many of these fighters carried much heavier armament than the fighters at the end of 1942 and were much more efficient at shooting down bombers.

VIII Bomber Command

In accordance with CBO and *Pointblank* priorities, VIII Bomber Command continued focusing on German fighter factories. The main production plants for the Bf 109s – in fact, for almost 50 percent of all German fighters – were at Regensburg and Wiener Neustadt. But Regensburg was 525 miles from England and Wiener Neustadt 725 miles, much too far for a normal mission for English-based VIII Bomber Command B-17s. The USAAF leadership decided that because of the distance, the Wiener Neustadt raid would be flown from North Africa by the two Ninth Air Force B-24 groups and the three B-24 groups from the Eighth. These were still in Africa on detached service in Libya, recuperating from the effects of the maximum-effort, low-level attack on the Ploesti oil fields that had taken place on August 1. The plan was that the B-24 groups would raid Wiener Neustadt, while on the same day the long-range B-17s of the 4th Wing would target Regensburg and split the defenses.

A Bf 110 *Zerstörer* with Wfr. Gr 21 rocket launchers. The *Zerstörer* were the most effective bomber destroyers but were not maneuverable and had to be kept away from the American escort fighters. (Bundesarchiv, Bild 101I-649-5370-41A, Fotograf: Hausmann)

An Me 410/U4 with a long-range 50mm cannon from II./ZG 26 "Horst Wessel" breaks off from an unusually close-range attack on a B-17. The large cannon had a propensity to jam and the pilot may have pressed in close trying to get a shot off. (NARA)

Both missions were planned for August 7, but on this and succeeding days the weather was not good enough for the Regensburg force to attack from England. Rather than wait for reliably good weather in the United Kingdom, on August 13 the B-24s from Africa attacked the Wiener Neustadt plants, supposedly one of the most heavily defended targets in Europe, without the benefit of the B-17s to divide the German fighter defenses. Fortunately, the Germans were caught by surprise due to the long distance involved and losses were much lighter than expected, while the bombing results were excellent.

Meanwhile, on August 12, VIII Bomber Command had sent 330 bombers to attack Bochum, Gelsenkirchen, and Bonn. The leading Fortress of the Gelsenkirchen force carried the famous movie star Clark Gable, a captain in the USAAF, who took film footage of the proceedings for use in a gunnery training film. Most of the missions were spoiled by weather and only two groups bombed their assigned objective, while others had to go for targets of opportunity. As the formations spread out, as usual the Luftwaffe took advantage of the disorganization. The 4th Wing suffered very few losses, but the 1st Wing groups met particularly heavy opposition from over 200 RLV fighter sorties. Twenty-five B-17s were shot down, a number surpassed only by the losses on June 13, but that record was soon to be shattered.

Mission 84

Even with the lost opportunity to fly the joint attack on Wiener Neustadt and Regensburg, VIII Bomber Command planners in the United Kingdom remained enamored with the idea of a complex attack to split the German defenses. Having missed one opportunity, they developed a plan for another simultaneous assault against both the Messerschmitt complex at Regensburg and the antifriction ball bearing industry at Schweinfurt. One hundred and forty-seven B-17s of 4th Wing, which had the long-range Fortresses with Tokyo tanks, would strike the Regensburg Messerschmitt factory and then turn south and fly on over the Alps to Allied bases in Algeria. This move was expected to confuse the enemy defenses, who would be expecting the force to return to the United Kingdom.

The second raid by the 1st Wing would follow the Regensburg force by ten minutes on a parallel track, then turn slightly to strike the ball bearing factories in the Schweinfurt area, and finally return to the English bases over the reciprocal of its route to the target. Because of the distances, neither force would have enough fuel to vary its course.

For weeks the weather was too bad for both the deep penetration into southern Germany and the subsequent flight to African bases, but when good weather was forecast beginning August 16, the decision was made to launch the dual missions the following morning, August 17.

It was expected that the raids would cause a large-scale air battle, so the escort would consist of all four operational P-47 groups – 18 squadrons of Thunderbolts, most equipped with the paper belly tanks – and 16 squadrons of Spitfires. With the expectation that the first raid on Regensburg would draw the bulk of the enemy fighters, the P-47s would escort the 4th Wing out to the limit of the Thunderbolts' range, and it was predicted that after the Germans attacked the 4th Wing they would not have time to land and refuel/rearm in time to meet the incoming Schweinfurt force just a few minutes behind. The P-47s would then return and refuel in time to meet the 1st Wing bombers returning to England after they bombed Schweinfurt.

The movie star Clark Gable flew five dangerous combat missions shooting film footage for the Army Air Force, including one where his B-17 was heavily damaged. He later starred in an excellent movie about Eighth Air Force bomber operations, "Command Decision." (NARA)

The two forces' take-off was scheduled for dawn, but morning fog at all the bases forced a delay. The fog at the bases of the 4th Wing destined for Regensburg broke early and, since the Regensburg portion could not be delayed for more than an hour so that the bombers could land at the African bases before dusk, VIII Bomber Command launched the 4th Wing immediately. The fog remained over 1st Division bases destined for Schweinfurt, so the chance for the two forces to go out together to split and confuse enemy defenses by a two-pronged thrust was lost.

The delay to the Schweinfurt force meant that both forces would have to fight their way in, so Eighth split the four groups of P-47s, two escorting the Regensburg force and two the delayed Schweinfurt force. VIII Bomber Command held the Schweinfurt task force for three-and-a-half hours after the Regensburg force had departed so that the P-47s supporting the Regensburg raid would have time to land, refuel, and support the return of the Schweinfurt raid.

Regensburg

The German controllers, warned of the raids by radio intercepts, were ready and waiting for the Regensburg raid. The 4th Wing bomber column consisted of three combat wings, the first combat wing with three groups, and the second and third with two groups each. As the raid crossed the coast, one P-47 fighter group arrived to escort the lead combat wing, but a timing mistake by the second P-47 group left it flying above the second combat wing, meaning the third combat wing was unescorted 15 miles behind the rest of the force and out of sight of the escorts. The German controllers quickly saw the gap and vectored the RLV fighters to the third wing which was out of sight of the Thunderbolts.

The RLV fighters began their head-on attacks on the third wing, mainly directed at the lowest group, and especially the low squadron of the low group, which suffered the heaviest

Leeuwarden

Schiphol

Deelen

Woensdrecht

Eindhoven

Brussels

Mönchengladbach

St Trond

Cologne

Vitry

Eupen

Koblenz

Lachen-Speyerdo

KEY

USAAF

B-17s

B-17s under attack

P-47 escorts

Luftwaffe

Airfields

EVENTS

1. 0600hrs. German controllers hear radio transmissions from the assembling US bomber force in England, and call for fighter forces from all over northern Europe to be sent down to attack the raid on its return leg.

2. 0800–0935hrs. 4th Bomb Wing takes off and forms up with only two fighter groups as escorts.

3. 1000hrs. The B-17s cross the coast.

4. 1005hrs. P-47 escorts arrive, timing mistake leaves rear B-17 wing unguarded. German fighters concentrate on the rear wing.

5. 1032hrs. Over Eupen, P-47 escorts leave.

5–6. 1015–1130hrs. Luftwaffe mass attacks over Holland and Germany. Thirteen B-17s shot down from last wing, 122 aircraft are left to bomb Regenburg.

7. Attack 1149–1207hrs. Bombing altitude was 17,000–20,000ft. Two groups reattack, and the bombing was excellent.

8. The turn south surprises the Germans, after which the force suffers no more losses.

9. (not visible) The force lands at US bases in French Algeria. The 4th Bomb Wing lost 14 B-17s over Europe, ten more at different points, for total losses of 24.

hafen

Jever

Oldenburg

Berlin

GERMANY

en-Erbenheim

Schweinfurt

m

Kitzingen

Fürth

6

7

8

Echterdingen

Regensburg

Munich

9

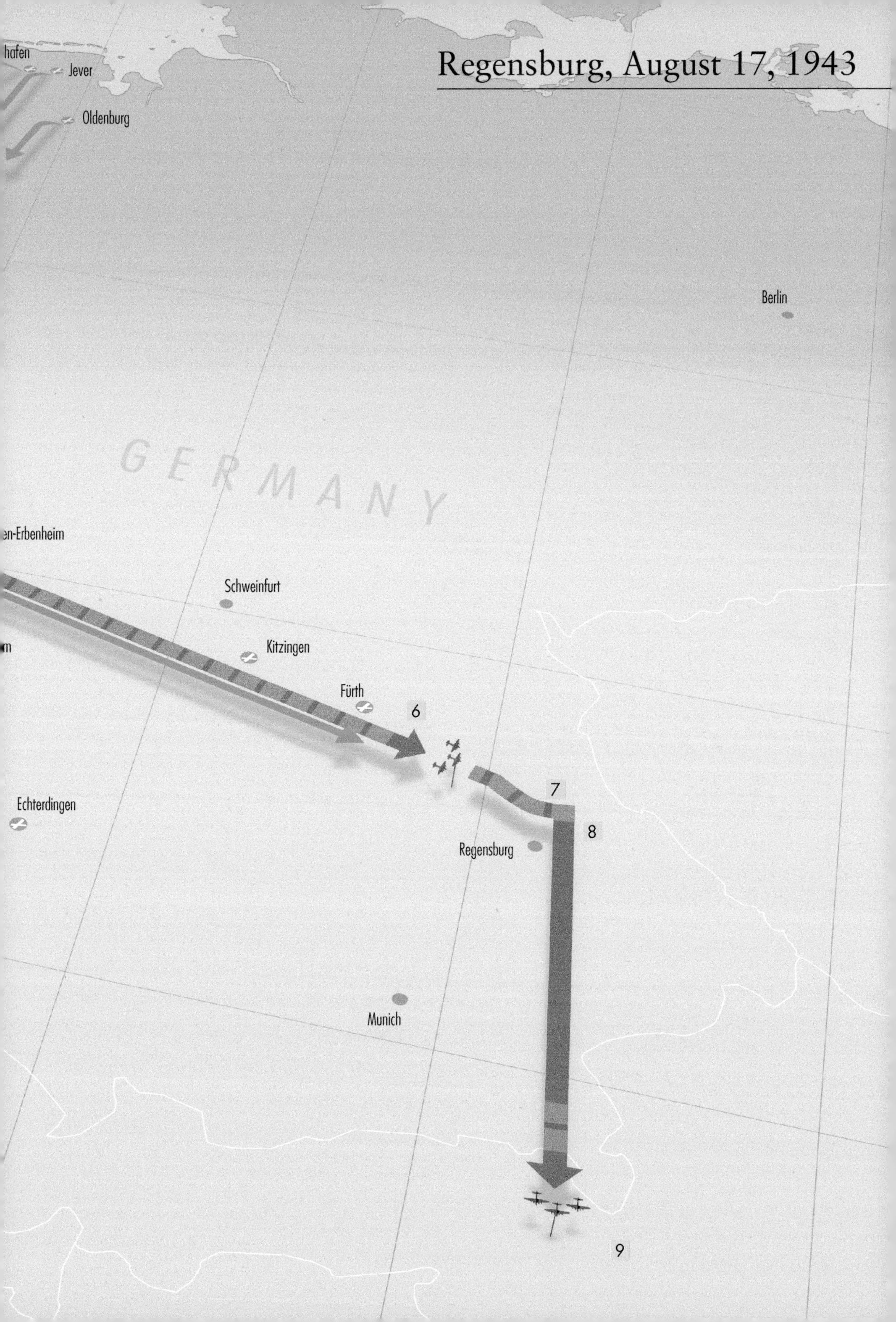

The bombing of the Bf 109 factory at Regensburg was one of most accurate American bombing raids of 1943, mainly because the bombing altitude was 10,000ft lower than normal for accuracy. After the bomb run the bombers turned south to American bases in Africa, briefly confusing the German controllers. (NARA)

losses. While the third combat wing was being battered, the Thunderbolts escorting the first two groups ran out of fuel and turned back, to see, to their dismay, B-17s going down from the third combat wing. The P-47 pilots, out of fuel, could only watch helplessly as the German pilots repeatedly pressed their attacks.

Once the escorts had left, the German fighters had a relatively easy time. The fighters usually ran out of fuel or ammunition after 30 minutes of combat, but there were so many bases along the route that the American force was attacked during virtually the entire run-in.

Of the 139 B-17s which had crossed the Dutch coast, 14 had been shot down, 13 from the last combat wing; two more had left their formations, released their bombs, and were flying south, hoping to cut a corner and catch up later; and one of the planes still with the formation had been forced to jettison its bomb load. This left 122 planes with bombs. The German fighters halted their attacks as the Fortresses reached the antiaircraft defenses over the target. Two of the groups in the leading combat wing had not been under serious attack and had so far suffered no casualties.

The clear weather and the wide loop of the River Danube made it easy to find the Regensburg Messerschmitt plant. The weather over the target was excellent, and Regensburg was such an important target that the raid had been ordered to fly 10,000ft lower than normal and bomb the targets at altitudes between 16,500ft and 19,250ft. The flak defenses were ineffective, so much so that one B-17 group that was not pleased with its run-in actually circled back to make another run. Bombing was excellent, heavily damaging the plant, killing 400 Messerschmitt workers, and destroying most of the fuselage jigs for the Me 262 jet fighter.

Then, as hoped, the RLV controllers were surprised when the force turned southwest and proceeded across the Alps and Italy, before making a maximum fuel-conserving flight over the Mediterranean to Tunisia. The force was harried by a few twin-engine Bf 110G night fighters, but they soon dropped off.

The Regensburg force lost 24 aircraft. Fourteen were shot down, two force-landed in Switzerland – the first battle-damaged USAAF warplanes to seek sanctuary there – four crash-landed in southern Europe, and four ditched in the Mediterranean off Tunisia. Most of the B-17s that were shot down were from the unescorted third combat wing, including ten from the 100th Group – the beginning of a long series of disasters that would lead to the group being called the "Bloody Hundredth."

Schweinfurt

Meanwhile, with the German controllers focused on the Regensburg raid, the German listening services monitoring VIII Bomber Command were surprised to hear the radio transmissions from the English bases that signaled another large-scale American bombing raid preparing to take off.

The Regensburg force's turn to Africa briefly confused the German controllers, but they quickly switched their attention to the four combat wings of the 1st Wing, 230 B-17s on their way to Schweinfurt three-and-a-half hours behind the Regensburg force. The limited range of the 1st Bomb Wing B-17Fs forced them to take the most direct route to Schweinfurt and back, almost precisely the route to Regensburg the 4th Wing had flown and the route the German controllers were expecting the Regensburg raid to use on the way back.

To intercept the returning raid on its expected return to England the controllers at the Jafü Holland–Ruhr control center had been sending fighters down from as far as the north German coast. Now, as the Germans detected that the remaining B-17s in England were assembling for their operation, these new forces landed to refuel on airfields near the inbound route for the delayed attack on Schweinfurt. The result was that the Germans had 13 of the 16 *Jagdgruppen* available to the RLV perfectly aligned to attack the Schweinfurt force.

The 1st Bomb Wing force that crossed into Europe was divided into two task forces of 12 groups, and from beginning to end was more than 20 miles in length. For the beginning of the mission it had a strong Spitfire escort, which negated the attacks of three of the *Gruppen* of RLV fighters, but the German controller still had ten *Gruppen* of single-engine fighters, about 200 single-engine fighters, some carrying Wfr. Gr. 21 rockets, supplemented by Bf 110G night fighters. This was the largest defensive force yet seen over Europe. The controllers had taken a gamble moving their units south and leaving the whole of northern Holland and northern Germany without any fighter cover at all, but the gamble paid off. At Antwerp the Spitfires withdrew and the bombers were picked up as scheduled by two groups of P-47s, but once again the escort plan fell apart because of a mistake by the leader of the first B-17 task force.

The plan was for the B-17s to fly at their normal altitude between 23,000ft and 26,500ft, and the escorting group, as normal, would fly slightly above them. But as the lead combat wing approached the coast its task force saw a cloud bank in front of them; so, deciding that his heavily laden bombers could not fly over the clouds, he elected to fly his entire B-17 force under them. The escort fighter group for the first combat wing approached the rendezvous point at the assigned altitude and tried in vain to locate the bombers below the clouds. The escort group never found the first force and had to return without engaging the Germans. The German controllers quickly saw this and followed their normal policy of attacking the weakest formations, sending the RLV fighters, including some Wfr. Gr. 21-firing Bf 109s, to attack the low group and the lead group of the first combat wing.

Outbound to Schweinfurt, August 17, 1943

A Holland-based Fw 190 bearing the colorful markings of II./JG 1 makes a head-on attack on a B-17F formation from the 91st Bomb Group, 1st Bombardment Wing, which was leading the first of two task forces on its way to Schweinfurt on August 17, 1943. The commander of the wing, Brigadier General Robert Williams, was the copilot on one of the aircraft in this formation, but both his aircraft and the lead aircraft survived the mission.

In the rear German Bf 110G night fighters are breaking off their attack. The fighters from II./JG 1 had been called down to intercept the Regensburg mission on its return flight, but when that mission turned to Africa these German fighters were in perfect position to intercept the 1st Bomb Wing when it made its weather-delayed attack on Schweinfurt, flying the same route as the Regensburg raid. The 91st Bomb Group B-17s are flying in fairly tight formation which provided good defensive firepower, but one of the bombers has already been hit in the cockpit area, and the formation gradually fell apart later in the raid as losses left gaps in the formation. The 1st Bomb Wing lost 36 B-17s on this raid, and the 91st lost seven of their 34.

Jim Laurier

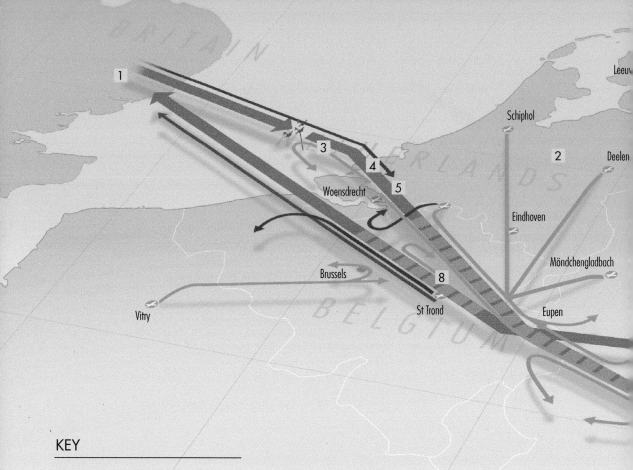

Leeuw

Schiphol

2

Deelen

Woensdrecht

Eindhoven

Möndchengladbach

Brussels

St Trond

Eupen

Vitry

1

3

4

5

8

KEY

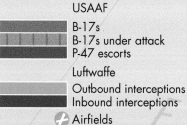

USAAF

B-17s
B-17s under attack
P-47 escorts

Luftwaffe

Outbound interceptions
Inbound interceptions

Airfields

BRITAIN

NETHERLANDS

BELGIUM

FRANCE

EVENTS

1. 0700hrs German listening units hear preparations in England for a second B-17 raid.

2. 0900–1100hrs. Alerted by the first raid, 260 German fighters arrive from all over western Europe to wait for the return of Regensburg force.

3. 1315–1400hrs. 1st Bomb Wing force takes off for Schweinfurt and crosses coast. Two P-47 groups escort force from Antwerp to Eupen.

4. 1410hrs. First B-17 group encounters clouds, drops down below them. P-47 escort group cannot find them.

5. 1415–1450hrs. German fighters attack now-unescorted first group near Antwerp and continue to Rhine. Come close to obliterating lead group, shooting down 21 B-17s.

6. 1450–1511hrs. Fighter attacks cease. At Schweinfurt 184 B-17s bomb the targets, and the bombing is reasonably good. As the force begins to return to England, 29 bombers have been lost.

7. 1530–1620hrs. Germans lose track of raid, then relocate it and send Bf 110 heavy night fighters to attack.

8. 1621hrs. US 56th Fighter Group overflies returning B 17 force and comes in behind it, surprising a large group of German fighters preparing to attack. 56th FG shoots down 11 German fighters, including four Bf 110 night fighters.

Schweinfurt, August 17, 1943

Wittmindhafen
Jever
Oldenburg
Rheine
ne
GERMANY
Koblenz
Weisbaden-Erbenheim
7
6
Schweinfurt
Mannheim
Lachen-Speyerdorf
Kitzingen
Fürth
Echterdingen
Regensburg
Munich

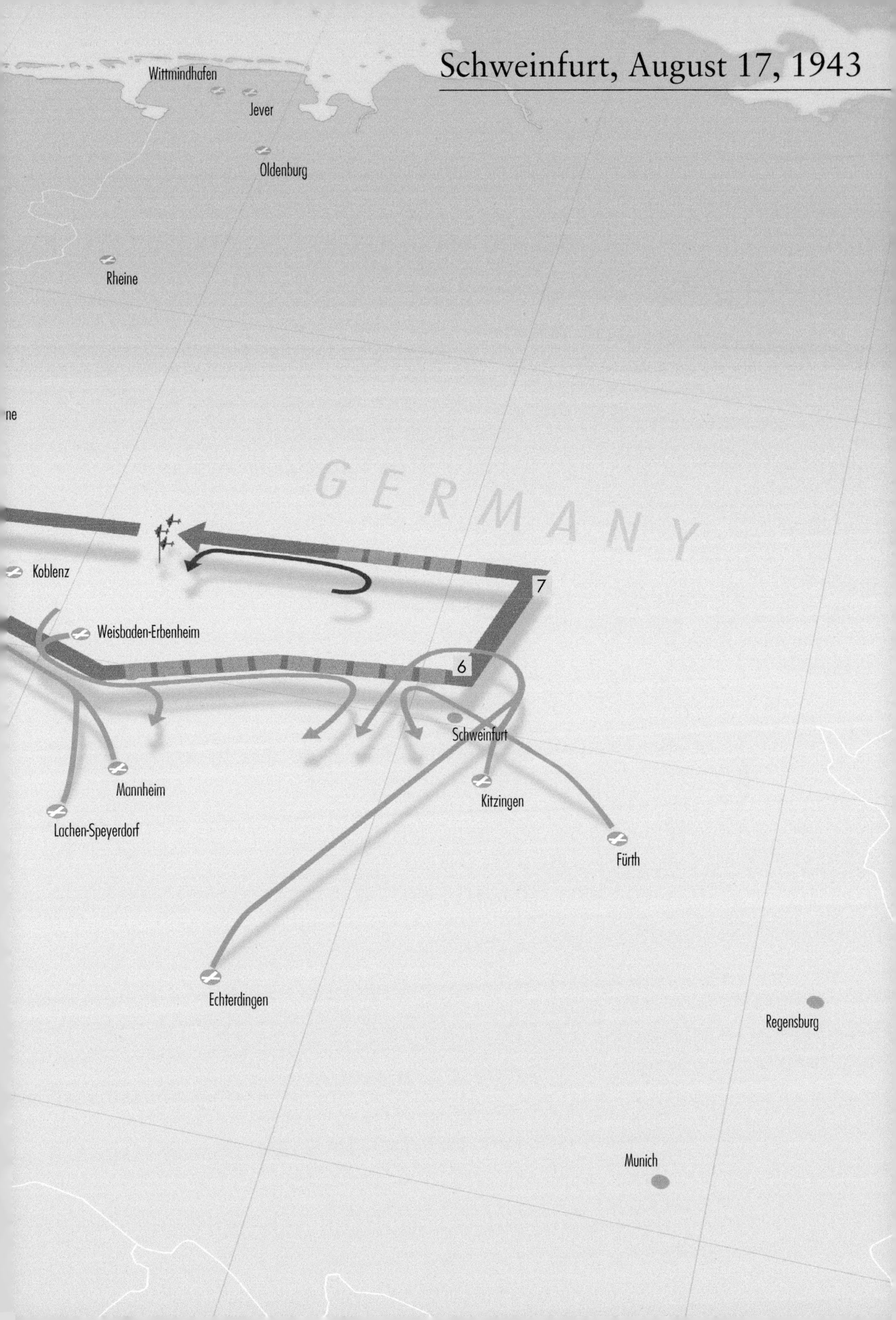

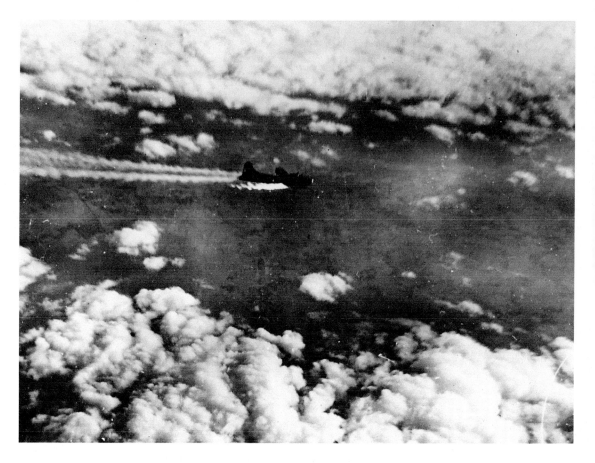

Later-model B-17Fs carried extra fuel in outer-wing "Tokyo tanks," but when the tanks were empty the fumes caught on fire very easily and made them very vulnerable as seen in this picture. The tanks were factory installed and could not be removed and the added range offset their extra vulnerability. (NARA)

The low group of the first combat wing took the initial brunt of the attacks; four of its five B-17s were shot down, as were almost half the bomb group just ahead of them. These were followed by attacks on the high squadron which shot down four of the eight B-17s. The high/high position, usually a safe spot, was then filled by another squadron, but that squadron was wiped out as well.

The P-47s escorting the second wing had kept them from being attacked, but they had to turn back at Eupen on the German border and for the next two hours the force was at the mercy of ten German fighter groups which concentrated on the first combat wing. Once the Germans began to attack the unescorted first half of the raid, they continued to concentrate on that combat wing, while the trailing second half of the bomber force, which had initially been escorted, lost very few aircraft.

The fighters broke off their attacks as the bombers approached Schweinfurt, but the bombing there was not as effective as at Regensburg, probably because the bombers flew at a higher altitude and those in the rear combat wings were hampered by smoke from the leading raids. Still, they did a great deal of damage. Plant records indicate 80 high-explosive hits on the two main bearing plants and that 663 machines were destroyed or damaged. Losses in the ball-bearing department were especially serious; there, production dropped from 140 tons in July to 69 in August and just 50 in September, and despite heavy demand output did not increase until November 1943.

As the raid began to head back to England, some of the RLV single-engine fighter pilots were exhausted from flying two sorties and many were scattered at fields to refuel, so only a relatively small number of single-engine fighters tried to intercept the returning force. Several Bf 110G night fighters began to attack the low group of the last combat wing but they used standard night fighter tactics for attacking RAF night bombers, coming in low behind the bombers and approaching to close range. The B-17 ball- and tail-gunners easily shot several down.

The P-47s of the 56th Fighter Group, scheduled to escort the returning bombers, had climbed out at a low, fuel-saving power setting and retained their external fuel tanks. They made the rendezvous point on time, but with the extra gas they had saved they overflew the B-17 formation to a point 15 miles beyond the German border, much farther east than the P-47s had ever flown before. They were undetected by several formations of German attackers below them who were concentrating on getting in position to attack, and the P-47s swung in behind the surprised RLV formations and shot down 16 German fighters, including at least five Bf 110G night fighters. These Bf 110Gs were a critical loss, not only of experienced crews but also of the aircraft and their scarce, sophisticated radar equipment.

Counting the cost

The overall cost of the two raids was 60 B-17s (the previous high was 26 on the June 13 raid), plus approximately 60 men dead and wounded in returning bombers. In the 1st Wing, 36 B-17s were lost, most from the leading wing. From the 4th Wing, 24 were lost to various causes.

To compound the 4th Wing's losses, because of the inadequate maintenance facilities in North Africa only 60 of the 115 Fortresses that reached Africa were ready to fly back immediately, and the lack of replacement parts and servicing equipment delayed the return of many of the other B-17s for some weeks.

The USAAF leadership had hoped that the flight of the Regensburg force to bases in North Africa would begin a program of regular shuttle bombing which would capitalize on the generally better weather prevailing in the Mediterranean area and on the confusion into which the maneuver was expected to plunge the enemy fighter control. But the raid showed that it was difficult to operate heavy bombers without their ground crews, especially if maintenance and base facilities were insufficient as they were in Africa. Moreover, landing away from their bases put an additional strain on combat crews and adversely affected their efficiency.

The German response

Strategically, this first attack on the antifriction bearing industry concerned Milch and Speer, and the German leaders began to investigate the possibilities of replacing high-quality or scarce bearings with those of simpler types which were plentiful, and to seek additional sources of finished stock in Sweden and Switzerland. The result was that the Germans were never short of antifriction bearings at any time during the war. This policy, soon expanded to other areas, made it possible for the Germans to avoid the dire consequences that would ordinarily follow heavy and accurate bombing of a highly concentrated industry, and they were helped – again – by the Americans' inability in 1943 to reattack the tough industrial targets because of heavy losses.

For the RLV, despite their success, there were complaints sent to Galland. Some units were formally accused of not making a concentrated (and dangerous) mass unit head-on attack. These units, which sought aircraft kills made possible by other units, were denounced as *Leichenfledderei* ("corpse-looters").

In response, Galland issued a sharp memo to all the single- and twin-engine fighter units engaging day-bomber formations:
1. Only bombers in formation are to be attacked, without regard for whether they are inbound or outbound.
2. Individual bombers are to be attacked only after the entire formation has been broken up or there is no other possibility of engagement.

3. *Nebelwerfer-Flugzeuge* [Wfr. Gr. 21 aircraft] are permitted to attack stragglers after successfully firing their rockets – no other exceptions allowed.

4. Formation leaders and pilots who violate these orders are subject to court-martial on the grounds of military disobedience with severe consequences to the security of the Reich.

Galland also ordered that attacks on enemy formations in *Geschwader* strength would be led by the *Geschwader* commander to give the pilots the example of a willingness to attack.

There were other equipment issues. Galland ordered an increase in the production of auxiliary fuel tanks to improve the fighters' range, as well as an increase in the number of *Fühlungshalter* using Bf 110s and Ju 88s with highly trained crews and the best navigational training and complete communications equipment. He also ordered more airfields designated as *Jagdstutzpunkte* (fighter support points) and instructed that all other airfields at least be provided with fuel to facilitate flying to the next *Jagdstutzpunkt*. For command and control a minimum of 12 aircraft per *Gruppe* were to be reequipped with the FuG 16ZY apparatus to support the Y-process.

Galland saw that the future success of the Reich defenses was based on the assumption that USAAF escorts had already reached their maximum range, but he realized after Schweinfurt that the escorts' range was creeping further into Germany. He feared that the Americans would soon be able to escort their heavy bombers with fighter aircraft to industrial targets deep inside Germany, and he tried to convince Göring of this. He pointed out that Thunderbolts had crossed the German border on the 17th and there was a P-47 wreck near Aachen. Göring became apoplectic and declared that the only possible reason could have been that the P-47

A German fighter closes to close range on a B-17 on fire, perhaps hit by flak. This attack on a crippled plane instead of reorganizing for another mass attack was an ongoing problem for the Luftwaffe. It was strongly criticized by Galland and Göring, to the point that they actually had commanders act as "commissars" to ensure that units did not pursue crippled planes but instead attacked the main force. (NARA)

An Fw 190 carrying Wfr. Gr. 21 tubes makes a follow-up gun attack on an American bomber. Goering ordered these rocket-armed single-seat fighters to attack the bombers after firing their rockets, even though their performance was drastically cut by the launch tubes. The tubes were jettisonable, but the jettison mechanism was not reliable. (NARA)

ran out of fuel at high altitude and glided into Germany, then gave Galland an order stating that "Allied fighters had never penetrated German airspace."

Adding to the controversy about the German air defenses, the night after Schweinfurt–Regensburg, RAF Bomber Command made a beautifully executed raid on the V-2 rocket testing facility at Peenemünde on the Baltic coast in northeast Germany, killing about 750 scientists and workers there and setting the V-2 project back by months. The defense effort was a fiasco, and the following night the Luftwaffe Chief of the General Staff, Hans Jeschonnek, committed suicide.

The suicide of Jeschonnek was a great boon to Galland and Milch, who believed that the increased penetration depth of the heavy bombers and the growing range of their fighters made it necessary to consider the entire Reich, including the western-occupied region, as a single defensive zone. Jeschonnek had been a believer in an offensive strategy, using the Luftwaffe in Russia and the Mediterranean, and had tried to block every attempt to switch Luftwaffe priorities to the defense of the homeland. Though Jeschonnek was out of favor when he died, his death helped Galland and Milch with their plans to shift the Luftwaffe's priorities to defending Germany. His replacement, General der Flieger Gunther Korten, was sympathetic to Galland and Milch.

Thunderbolt interception, August 17, 1943

While covering the return of the Schweinfurt raid of August 17, 1943, the 56th Fighter Group led by Colonel "Hub" Zemke flew at a very economical fuel setting and was able to fly deeper into Germany than P-47s had ever flown before. The group actually overflew the exiting B-17 force and came around behind a large force of German fighters. The P-47s shot down several single-seat fighters and also caught a group of German Bf 110G night fighters. Here Lieutenant Frank McCauley from the 61st Fighter Squadron, flying his P-47D *Rat Racer*, shoots down a Bf 110G from I./NJG 4 at about 1530hrs, one of 21 of the night fighters the Germans lost that day. These German night fighters had attacked the raid both on the way in and on the way out, but they were manned by inexperienced crews that had not scored many night kills yet and their rear-firing defensive weapons consisted of only one or two small-caliber machine guns. Nevertheless, the night fighters were a very valuable commodity because of their expensive radar equipment, and the German night-fighter crews who rarely saw a bomber were awestruck by "the overwhelming strength of the enemy air forces attacking our country."

Another picture of a 4th Bomb Wing B-17F with a fire in its "Tokyo tanks." The Germans knew from captured B-17s this was a vulnerable spot but to hit it the B-17 usually had to be attacked from behind, a much more dangerous angle than a head-on attack. (NARA)

VIII Bomber Command's September reinforcement

Beginning in the fall of 1943, USAAF commander General Arnold's decision to give Eighth Air Force priority resulted in a huge influx of new bombers; the number of aircraft in heavy bombardment groups was increased from 35 to 62 planes, and now groups could fly two group boxes on a single mission. Additionally, in early September the Eighth's three B-24 groups were back in England and a new group also arrived, bringing B-24 strength to four groups, while B-17 strength had increased to 16 combat groups. There were now six P-47 groups, two more than had been available on August 17, and there were also sufficient numbers of the very useful 75- or 108-gallon pressurized drop tanks.

A new Fortress model, the B-17G, began to reach squadrons in the form of replacement aircraft during September. It carried a Bendix remotely controlled "chin" turret, introduced on the YB-40 and found very useful for forward defense; it also gave the bombardier more room to operate. It had the same power as the B-17F but was heavier and thus slower; however, with the additional room in the nose it quickly became the preferred model for the lead crews.

Some late-production B-17Fs were also fitted with this turret, but the majority of F models soldiered on in their original form until shot down or retired. The average life expectancy of an Eighth Air Force Fortress in late 1943 was only 11 missions, but over a dozen original B-17Fs of the pioneer groups survived until they were finally replaced by B-17Gs.

Now that General Arnold had ensured Eighth Air Force received the bulk of the new equipment, understandably he pressed for results. However, the best (if not most deadly) defense of German industry against attack from the American bombers was cloud cover, which prevented any major strikes at German targets for the remainder of August and early September.

Finally, on September 6 the weather improved marginally and, yielding to Arnold's pressure, VIII Bomber Command launched a raid of over 400 bombers, including a diversion force of B-24s recently returned from Africa, flying their first combat mission since their return. The main force was the largest sent out so far, with 388 B-17s led by the 4th Bomb Wing to attack the Bosch instrument factory in Stuttgart, where 90 percent of Germany's magnetos and fuel injection nozzles were being produced. This was the first daylight attack on Stuttgart and the round-trip distance was 1,300 miles, close to the absolute limit of the 1st Bomb Wing's early-model B-17F's range. The force was escorted by 176 P-47s.

The mission was a disaster. The weather deteriorated as the force passed through France on the way to the target and scattered many of the B-17 formations, but the RLV fighter force, also hampered by weather, was slow to react. However, once inside Germany the RLV fighters from the interior bases were able to launch against the 4th Wing. The first head-on fighter attacks concentrated on the low box, brought down 11 B-17s from the group, and completely wiped out the squadron on "Purple Heart Corner."

When the leading 4th Wing groups reached the target they found it almost completely covered with clouds. The mission commander elected to circle the target for almost 30 minutes with the bomb-bay doors open, burning fuel, but in the end only one combat wing bombed in the target area. The bomber force then broke up to seek targets of opportunity – 233 dropped on such targets – but the separate formations continued to be attacked by RLV fighters.

The 1st Bomb Wing was scattered and struggled to find targets, and some of the B-17s flew past the original target and climbed to higher altitude looking for something cloud-free to bomb. This made for a very long flight back; many of the shorter-range Fortresses of the 1st Wing did not have the long-range "Tokyo tanks" and were lost directly or indirectly to fuel shortage. In all 45 bombers were lost, with many others scrapped upon their return. Twelve B-17s had to ditch in the English Channel, but all of the crews were picked up by the very effective RAF rescue boats. Five landed in Switzerland and eight had to land on English country fields.

Beginning September 9, to the chagrin of the Eighth Air Force leadership, a number of missions were flown into France to support Operation *Starkey*, a mock invasion of France.

Reorganization

With its growth, VIII Bomber Command reorganized. On September 13 it added an air division between VIII Bomber Command and the wings, and the 1st, 2nd, and 4th Bombardment Wings were renamed 1st, 2nd, and 3rd Bombardment Divisions respectively. The 1st and 3rd Divisions were B-17s and the 2nd Division was B-24s.

In actuality the changes were simply ones of designation for existing organizations. They continued to function in much the same fashion, from the same bases and with the same commanders, and the term "combat wing" remained in use for the battle formation composed of two or three group boxes.

Weather changes

The weather problems gradually brought some changes. There were small-scale night bombing trials within VIII Bomber Command and one squadron practiced night flights during the late summer of 1943. Several times in September B-17s accompanied an RAF force bombing German cities, but the missions made it clear that the B-17 was not an effective night bomber.

A more promising avenue for striking in bad weather was the RAF's blind-bombing and navigational aids, including the short-range precision navigation device *Oboe* and the ground-scanning *H2S*, which was particularly effective in showing the distinction between water and land, and therefore picking up the rough outline of a particular city. But both *Oboe*

What appears to be a controlled bailout from a 95th BG B-17, probably over the English Channel, where RAF rescue launches were almost certain to pick up downed crew members. (NARA)

and *H2S* were in short supply. A special unit was formed, the 482nd Group (Pathfinder), to fly lead position in a combat wing, with all bombers dropping on its release. British smoke marker bombs would be used to mark the release point for following formations.

The first mission was on August 27, when four B-17Fs of the new Pathfinder Force (PFF) led an attack against the port of Emden. Only one of the *H2S* systems functioned properly but the formation achieved a fair concentration of bombs on Emden; however, later *H2S* missions were less successful and it was clear that more training in *H2S* bombing was needed to make it useful. The American *H2X* version was developed, but it was not until 1944 that instrument bombing really became a part of VIII Bomber Command's arsenal.

German reinforcement

By mid-September the Luftwaffe was completely focused on defending the Reich and had drastically cut ground attack operations in Russia and the Mediterranean. The number of single-engine fighters facing the Eighth Air Force rose from approximately 300 in April to nearly 800 in October, about 65 percent of total German fighter strength. The bulk of this defense force – the equivalent of 19 *Jagdgruppen* – was concentrated in Germany. The most important new additions were the twin-engine Bf 110 and Me 410 day fighters with heavy cannon armament and, most importantly, four Wfr. Gr. 21 rocket launchers on each aircraft. This 21cm rocket missile had proven extremely effective in breaking up the tight formations and was being employed more extensively, and the Bf 110 and Me 410 *Zerstörer* had been found to be excellent launch vehicles. There were now two *Zerstörer* groups with 60 twin-engine fighters available, while 16 night fighter *Gruppen* could also be called upon in an emergency.

All the Fw 190s and Bf 109s were now equipped with racks for external fuel tanks and could travel 250 miles from base to join the battle. The cowl-mounted 7.92mm machine guns on both aircraft had been replaced by 13mm machine guns, and extra 20mm and the very effective MK 108 30mm cannon were added specifically for "killing Boeings," with some carrying two Wfr. Gr. 21s.

The October battles

Making the escorts more effective was now an urgent priority for the Eighth Air Force. Since June USAAF commander General Arnold had criticized Eaker for his use of escort fighters, but as Eaker was his friend he instead fired the head of VIII Fighter Command, General Hunter, and replaced him with Major General William Kepner, over Eaker's objections. Kepner had worked closely with the fighter manufacturers to increase the range of the USAAF fighters and was considered innovative, energetic, and aggressive. He was to prove to be an excellent fit for his new job.

Eaker continued to be under pressure from Arnold to show more results. With the approach of the long European winter that could virtually shut down daylight bombing operations, Eaker and his bomber commander, Major General Fred Anderson, decided on a compressed series of maximum-strength missions to high-priority targets, most deep in Germany and thus far beyond the range of the available escorts.

The first clear weather mission of October took place on October 4 when 361 B-17s bombed a number of targets, with the 1st Bomb Division making the main thrust at Frankfurt-am-

A Bf 109G carrying two extra 20mm Mauser MG 151/20 underwing gun pods in its *Rüstsätze* (field modification). These more than doubled its firepower for attacking bombers but adversely affected the Bf 109's performance much more than it did the larger Fw 190. (Bundesarchiv, Bild 101I-662-6659-38, Fotograf: Hebenstreit)

A P-47 attacks a virtually helpless Bf 110 rocket-firing Zerstörer, a situation the German controllers tried to avoid at all costs. In the fall of 1943 the German successes were based on keeping the Zerstörer out of range of the escorts, which became more and more difficult as the P-47s received improved external fuel tanks that increased their range. (NARA)

Main while the 3rd Division attacked targets in the Saar. The German single-seat fighters were unusually ineffective, shooting down only 12 B-17s and not flying any second sorties as the force withdrew. To add to the American success, the 56th Fighter Group P-47s pounced on a flight of Bf 110 Zerstörer and shot down nine of them, showing again the vulnerability to escorts of the Zerstörer, and overall the RLV lost 23 fighters. A decoy mission flown by two groups of B-24s did suffer when they were attacked by single-engine fighters and rocket-armed Zerstörer, and four B-24s were shot down.

German air defense conference: October 1943

Göring was very unhappy with the RLV's performance on October 4, and was also upset by a message from the Frankfurt *Gauleiter*, one of the powerful Nazi district governors, complaining that the Americans flew over the city in "Nuremberg Party Rally" formations. On October 7–8, while some of the heaviest air battles raged, he convened a major conference of his fighter leaders to discuss all the issues with the Luftwaffe's day air defenses.

The agitated Göring opened with a screed on fighter-pilot morale, training, tactics, and weaknesses of German fighter technology, and in the process said that Luftwaffe veteran pilots were, in effect, worn-out cowards.

He issued a set of orders (many of which were apparently ignored):

- There are no weather conditions in which fighter units cannot take off and engage in combat.
- Any fighter pilot returning to base with neither a combat victory nor combat damage will be court-martialed.
- Any fighter pilot whose armament fails is expected to ram.

Göring also emphasized that German fighters had to rearm and refuel quickly so they could engage deep USAAF penetrations two or possibly three times, and ordered all this to become standing policy.

While the fighter leaders chafed under the criticism, they knew Göring had a point. Successfully attacking the American bomber forces required that their formations be broken up, and for single-engine fighters this meant mass head-on attacks on the bomber formations pressed to very close range; many pilots did not possess the nerve for this level of close-range combat.

To make sure the formation leaders carried out these attacks properly, Galland ordered the fighter commanders to fly missions as "flying commissars" and observe the degree of determination with which their units attacked. Galland also ordered the installation of gun cameras in the fighters so that after each mission the film could be examined to make sure they were pressing their head-on attacks to close range. An order dated October 7 formalized all these requirements, though they were often disregarded.

While the conference was continuing, on October 8 VIII Bomber Command launched a three-pronged attack on Bremen. The 3rd Division approached from the northwest over the

North Sea, while the 1st Division made a more direct approach across Holland and the 2nd Division, with 55 B-24 Liberators, went another North Sea route and descended to attack Vegesack. Withdrawal for all B-17s was to be across Holland, while the B-24s returned by much the same route as they had come, far out in the North Sea.

The divergent courses did not fool the German controllers, and both the B-17 divisions came under heavy attack when the P-47 escort had turned back. Fw 190s and Bf 109s used the familiar pattern of attack on the leading elements of 1st Division, whose groups had led the Schweinfurt raid and suffered so highly in August, and who once again were the target. The division was also attacked by rocket-firing Bf 110 *Zerstörer*. When the P-47s met the force on the way back, the low group of the division had lost seven of its 18 bombers, including the lead aircraft, and all its remaining bombers received some damage.

Meanwhile, 3rd Bomb Division was also heavily attacked. When the one of the groups lost both its leader and deputy to flak, the formation spread out and the RLV fighters, always looking for the loosest formations, shot down half the division, seven B-17s, and overall 30 B-17s were lost.

On this mission Eighth Air Force adopted another British radio device, code-named *Carpet*, which the RAF had used for some time to jam the flak gun-laying radar. Forty B-17s of the leading 3rd Division groups used this equipment over Bremen with apparent success as they suffered least of the division's formations in the flak barrage. *Carpet* was gradually installed in many other bombers during the months ahead.

On October 9, despite the loss of 30 bombers and damage to over half the remainder on the Bremen–Vegesack mission, VIII Bomber Command began four days of major strikes deep into Germany, sending out 378 bombers to the most distant targets yet attempted. Flying over the North Sea and across Denmark, 150 bombers hit the port facilities and German naval units at Gdynia and submarine slips at Danzig. Another force of about 100

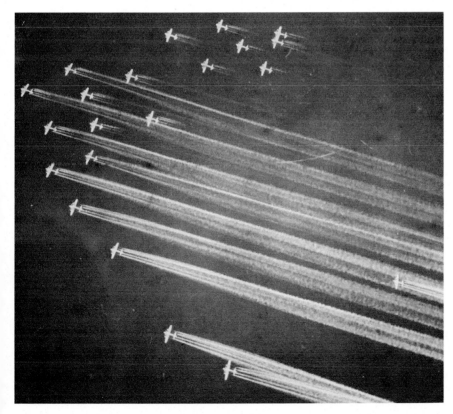

One very discouraging thing for German civilians was to see on a daily basis American bombers in a seemingly impeccable "Nuremberg Rally formation." (NARA)

An Fw 190 making a modified head-on attack on a B-17 formation. This pass was made when the fighter did not have enough time to line up properly for an attack from head on, which was sometimes difficult if the bomber formation turned. (NARA)

An Fw 190 breaks down and away from a B-17 formation after making a head-on pass on the formation in front of them. The "split S" breakaway was the common ending for a head-on pass, allowing the attacking fighter to build up speed to climb back up ahead of the bombers to make another head-on pass. (NARA)

bombers followed a similar route into East Prussia to attack the Focke-Wulf assembly plant at Marienburg and the Arado aircraft factory at Anklam as a diversion to pin down the RLV and keep it away from the bombers attacking the northern targets. It succeeded – the main force lost only ten bombers – but the diversion force had 18 bombers shot down.

That day Adolf Galland flew on the mission acting as a "flying commissar." Galland thought that attacks on the bombers with guns were disorganized and broken off too soon. On his return flight, Galland concluded that the Luftwaffe pilots were exhausted after flying a long second sortie, and from his own observation he knew what requirements were reasonable, which he hoped would make his discussions with Göring carry more weight. However, he had to concede that Göring was right in many respects – *Viermotschreck* was a problem.

The bombing was exceptionally good. The Arado Fw 190 components factory at Anklam suffered damage to virtually all its buildings and there was heavy damage at the port of Gdynia, but the 100 bombers that hit the Focke-Wulf plant at Marienburg provided the most spectacular results. The force bombed at the relatively low altitude of 11,000–14,500ft and almost half the bombs hit in the factory area, virtually wiping out the plant.

In fact, bombing accuracy for VIII Bomber Command had been steadily improving. In July 1943 VIII Bomber Command as a whole placed only 12.7 percent of its bombs within 1,000ft of the aiming point and 36.7 percent within 2,000ft, but by October these figures had been raised to 27.2 and 53.8 percent, respectively.

Much of this was certainly because the crews were more experienced and the selection process for lead crews had steadily improved, while the lead crew idea was integrated into bombardier training both in England and the United States during the summer and early fall. Additionally, tactics were constantly being revised to improve the accuracy of the last formations over the targets. In the first half of 1943 the first two formations over the targets had placed, respectively, 26.4 and 15.7 percent of their bomb tonnage within 1,000ft of the aiming point, whereas those in the third and fourth positions had succeeded in dropping only 9.7 and 7.8 percent in that area. By September the tactics had been revised so the formations were more spread out and, while there had been little improvement in the first formations, the third and fourth formations had improved by 58 and 105 percent;

formations still farther back showed improvement amounting to as much as 178 percent.

As for losses, those for the October 9 raid were 8 percent of the attacking force, but that spoke more for the element of surprise than the ability of the bombers, unescorted, to defend themselves. It was the diversionary force that drew the bulk of enemy attention and lost 17 percent of the force.

On October 10, a large high-pressure area was predicted to bring cloudless skies to Germany, permitting a broad choice of targets, and the forecast was as significant to the German planners as it was to the Americans. Assuming that the Eighth Air Force bombers would return to Germany on the 10th, three *Jagdgruppen* were moved overnight to the Dutch border where the normal American route was, and in the early morning of that day the large volume of radio traffic from the American bomber bases showed the Luftwaffe had guessed correctly.

While a head-on pass was the least dangerous way to attack a bomber formation, the formation still had a number of guns firing forward. Here an Fw 190 has been hit and damaged after making a head-on pass through a B-17 formation. (NARA)

It was indeed a heavy raid – 274 B-17s and 216 escorting P-47s – but it was a short raid to Münster, where the entire force could be escorted to the target. The aiming point for the B-17s would be Münster's distinctive cathedral in the heart of the city. This was the first time that the Eighth Air Force had specifically targeted civilians, the employees of one of the largest railroad switching yards serving the Ruhr, but when the crews were told they were being sent to kill and "dehouse" civilians it did not produce any moral qualms – indeed, many crew members cheered this news at the briefing.

The bombers flew a direct route to the target since they expected fighter escort all the way, but again a careful American plan and what should have been an easy mission was spoiled by the English weather, poor American execution, and German competence. The P-47 group that was to cover the leading bombers was late and another P-47 group was fogbound in the United Kingdom, so the leading 3rd Division bombers were unescorted for a period. This small lapse was quickly exploited by a German controller, and six *Jagdgruppen* began head-on attacks on the leading 4th Bomb Wing's three groups while Me 410s and Bf 110s launched rocket attacks on the rear.

Within seven minutes, virtually the entire low group was destroyed. Six B-17s had been quickly shot down, six others were so badly damaged that they dropped and were soon shot down, and only one of the group's 13 B-17s returned to England. Nearly half of another group's formation was shot down, and a quarter of a third group had also gone, with the entire leading wing on the verge of being totally wiped out, when P-47s of the 56th Group arrived to begin their withdrawal escort. By that time 29 B-17s from the 3rd Division had been shot down, 25 of those from the lead wing.

The 1st Division's P-47 escort group arrived exactly on schedule and began an incident-free escort of the division which sustained only one loss on the mission. The main air battle was far ahead of them. In the end the German fighters had shot down 30 B-17s, but the escorts had accounted for 25 German fighters and nine of the German losses were twin-engine *Zerstörer*, proving again that these would have to remain out of the way of the American escort.

The Germans were now involved in a war of attrition, and no matter how many kills they scored, they never turned back a full bombing raid. Concentration on a single bomber *Pulk* was a very effective tactic that would be repeated, but on this day, even though the *Pulk* chosen for attack was leading the mission, its near-destruction did not upset the bombing plan and the remaining bombers succeeded in making an effective attack on their target.

The spectacularly accurate "bombing of the year" was carried out on the Focke-Wulf factory at Marienburg on October 9, 1943. It was the farthest east that VIII Bomber Command had struck up until that point. (NARA)

On the American side, the losses drove the morale in the Eighth Air Force Bomber Command down very low. For one group, the 100th, Münster was another black chapter to add to an already grim book. The group had lost 20 bombers and over 200 men missing or killed in a week – including two squadron commanders.

There were rumors that the Luftwaffe had a vendetta against the 100th, but a postwar review of RLV records showed it was simply bad luck – on those missions on which they suffered heavy losses the 100th simply flew the position that bore the brunt of Luftwaffe attacks.

These October air battles over Germany also gave evidence of the increasingly effective use being made by the Luftwaffe of Wfr. Gr. 21 rockets. On August 2, 1943 the RLV had directed that the newly arrived Bf 110s and Me 410 *Zerstörer* should be fitted with two Wfr. Gr. 21 launchers under each wing. On August 15, the first Bf 110G-2 had been fitted with the weapons and the Me 410s quickly followed. Rockets had caused serious damage to the American *Pulks* in the Bremen battle and again over Anklam, but these were carried by Fw 190s and Bf 109s which, after lobbing them into the bomber formation, resumed operations as standard fighters.

But it was not until the second mission to the ball-bearing plants at Schweinfurt on 14 October that the Luftwaffe unleashed a really large-scale rocket attack completely coordinated with other fighter tactics. After the war, the July 1947 United States Strategic Bombing Survey noted:

A chaplain and his assistant watching a mission return. (NARA)

By the summer of 1943, twin-engine fighters were equipped with multiple rocket projectors of large caliber, firing time-fuzed rockets. These rocket-firing twins were found to be highly lethal to bombers when fired in salvo from a formation... All these attacks were planned for execution beyond Allied escort range since these aircraft were no match for our fighters. Their success in the fall of 1943 then appeared to be the answer to Allied bomber formations. On the vital penetrations to targets deep in Germany, US superiority in the air in daylight was put in serious doubt.

Second Schweinfurt: Mission 115, October 14

Despite the recent heavy losses, with a forecast of good weather on October 14 VIII Bomber Command scheduled a maximum effort return trip to Schweinfurt. All three bomb divisions were scheduled to fly the mission, and the Eighth hoped to send 360 B-17s and 60 B-24s, but losses from missions earlier in the month cut into this figure so only 291 B-17s actually launched. Since the route of the B-17s was beyond the normal combat radius of non-"Tokyo tank" B-17Fs, those planes had to carry one bomb bay fuel tank.

The force was dispatched in three forces, with 149 B-17s from the 1st Bombardment Division and 142 B-17s with Tokyo tanks from the 3rd Bombardment Division. The formations would cross enemy defenses roughly abreast, though some 30 miles apart, and then the courses would diverge slightly for deception. The plan called for the 1st Bomb Division to lead the train of bombers, followed by the 3rd Bomb Division which was on a parallel course just 10 miles to the south. As the B-17s approached Germany, almost 40 had aborted for various reasons. Because of the long distance to Schweinfurt, the B-17s had to fly a straight line to the target, which would make the German controllers' job easier. A third force of B-24s from the 2nd Bombardment Division was to fly a route to the south for a diversionary mission.

Each force, including the B-24s, was assigned one group of P-47s to escort the bombers to the maximum fighter range and one additional group of P-47s for withdrawal support from Eupen inland to mid-English Channel. This fighter escort was only a little stronger and with no greater range than the escorts on August 17. One group of long-range P-38s had just arrived in the United Kingdom from North Africa, and VIII Fighter Command hoped they could fly and would sweep the area ahead of the penetration and counter the *Zerstörer*, but they did not become operational until the following day.

The Germans were, as usual, alerted by their listening posts; the chief controller of the Holland center put his fighters on full alert and was calling down additional fighters 50 minutes before the American force approached the Dutch coast. By the time the B-17s crossed the coast, the RLV had about 150 single-engine fighters ready, and every rocket-firing Bf 110 and Me 410 *Zerstörer* unit in Germany had been called to join in the fray.

On the American side, the mission went badly from the beginning. When the 149 B-17s of the 1st Bomb Division took off, bad weather in the assembly route prevented one group

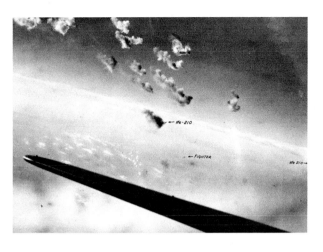

An interesting picture showing explosions from a Wfr. Gr. 21 rocket attack from two launching Me 410s (incorrectly identified as Me 210s) in the center of the picture and an Fw 190 well to their rear, perhaps preparing to launch more rockets. (NARA)

Airborne rocket attack, October 14, 1943

Four Bf 110Gs from I./ZG 26 attack the low box of B-17s from the 305th Group, 1st Bomb Division on the second Schweinfurt raid on October 14, 1943, about 1300hrs. The 305th Group lost 16 B-17s on this raid. The Bf 110Gs' tactic was to attack from slightly below the B-17 box and, after firing their 16 Wfr. Gr. 21 rockets – four per aircraft – at a range of about 1,000 yards, then break off to keep away from the B-17s' tail gunners. The Wfr. Gr. 21 was a converted spin-stabilized infantry rocket that had a very low launch velocity and thus had to be "lobbed" into the bomber formation from large upward-slanted tubes. The drag of these tubes severely reduced the Bf 110s' already limited performance. The fuses on the rockets had to be preset on the ground and, since the launch range had to be estimated, the rockets were inaccurate, but they were only intended to break up the bomber formations. However, the rockets had a blast area of 100ft, and American bomber crews considered them by far the most dangerous German airborne weapon. Both the Americans and the Germans knew that these twin-engine rocket-firing fighters, the Bf 110 and the Me 410, were extremely vulnerable to escort fighters, but in fall 1943 the Americans did not have a fighter with the range to threaten them.

from taking its planned position as the low group of the lead wing. Then, without telling the task force commander, this group joined as the low group of the following combat wing, forcing two groups to fly a combined high formation. This left the lead combat wing with only two groups, which was too vulnerable a force to lead the mission, so the task force commander took position behind the full wing, creating a very unwieldy formation. To make matters worse, bad weather and other difficulties meant that only 29 B-24s were available for a diversionary mission, which they cut short and did not distract the German defenses, while wasting the full P-47 group they took with them.

The 1st Division B-17s crossed the Dutch coast on a less direct route to Schweinfurt but the first turn by the 1st Division's five groups of B-17s strung the entire wing out, setting it up perfectly for the German fighters. However, the Germans also made mistakes in the beginning. The first wave of RLV fighters attacked before the P-47 escort had turned back, and the Germans were repulsed easily. But the German controllers moved the rest of their fighters back to just beyond Eupen, where the P-47s had to turn back, after which the RLV made its appearance in force and began to attack the bomber formations.

German tactics repeated the successful pattern developed previously in late August when the twin-engine *Zerstörer* joined the force. Most of the rocket-firing *Zerstörer* units reached the bombers well before they arrived at Schweinfurt and made their first attacks from the rear, destroying or damaging a few bombers, but most importantly the rocket explosions spread out the formations of the combat boxes, thus making the attacks by the large number of single-engine fighters easier. Some single-engine fighters also carried rockets, usually in the ratio of one *Staffel* per *Gruppe*, and these made gun attacks after they fired their rockets.

All of the German pilots were under orders to keep attacking until forced to withdraw by damage or shortage of fuel or ammunition. Most of the single-engine fighters attacked in columns from the front, singling out the most scattered and vulnerable formations of the stream. The better *Jagdgruppen* reorganized and made repeated head-on attacks, but many formation leaders settled for beam attacks, which were less demanding for the German pilots, but were much less successful.

This day it was the group in the low position and widely separated – the Germans noted, "in no recognizable formation" – that suffered, and 13 of its 16 B-17s were lost prior to the bomb run. The high group fared little better, losing ten aircraft before the target, and half the starting force – 27 B-17s of the first combat wing – were gone before the target. The leading unit lost seven of its 49 planes, and several more were so seriously damaged that they were soon to become part of the total of 29 lost by that formation.

The final destruction of damaged bombers that had left their formations was supposed to be left to the day and night twin-engine fighters, but single-engine pilots often made repeated attacks on bombers that they had already damaged, sometimes following them far enough to witness their crashes. Other single-engine pilots would disappear after their first closely monitored frontal pass on the close-packed bombers and spend the rest of their mission seeking out stragglers.

Unlike the 1st Division, the following 3rd Division was well organized, and its force of 142 B-17s had Tokyo tanks and could vary their route. They made a turn south that seemed to confuse the German controllers, and the division was not intercepted until it was well into Germany. The fighter attacks on this division did not begin until just before the bomb run and only the leading group took losses before the target.

The 3rd Division was six minutes behind the 1st Division, and its bombardiers had to deal with clouds of smoke caused by the preceding attack. Nevertheless, three of the five ball-bearing plants at Schweinfurt were bombed and all heavily hit, 88 bombs scoring direct hits on the factory buildings.

After leaving the target, the bombers made a wide turn south before taking the westerly route home in an attempt to confuse the enemy and stretch the range of his fighters, but the single-engine fighters continued to make heavy attacks, as did Bf 110s and Ju 88s from six night fighter *Geschwader*. The night fighters' operational-training unit reached the bombers just after "bombs away" and remained with the stream, claiming four B-17s shot down, the largest and most successful daylight operation ever flown by the twin-engine night fighters. The Luftwaffe eventually flew 833 sorties, with virtually every Luftwaffe fighter unit in western Europe joining in the battle.

The clouds that had so disrupted the Americans' formations over England in the morning grew thicker during the day and prevented the American fighters scheduled to be withdrawal escorts from taking off, but the weather moved across the Channel and also prevented many RLV units from flying a second mission, probably saving many B-17s in the shattered formations.

In all, 60 B-17s were destroyed by the Luftwaffe in almost three-and-a-half hours of continuous attacks, and 17 more bombers were scrapped. Only one group in VIII Bomber Command suffered neither casualties nor aircraft loss – the usually hard luck "Bloody

An unusual, probably staged shot of a four-ship Bf 110 *Zerstörer* formation, each armed with four Wfr. Gr. 21 rocket tubes, extra fuel tanks, and two extra 20mm cannon in the belly. (Bundesarchiv, Bild 1011-663-6734-10, Fotograf: Hebenstreit.)

A B-17 going down with fire in its Tokyo tanks while still under attack by an Fw 190. The Fw 190 was violating orders by attacking a single B-17 instead of trying to break up the formation. (NARA)

Hundredth". As usual, the B-17 gunners exaggerated, claiming 288 "confirmed" fighters downed. The Luftwaffe actually lost 53 aircraft.

Aftermath

Those in charge of Eighth Air Force operations overestimated the degree of lasting damage inflicted on the Schweinfurt plants and it was generally felt, both in Eighth Air Force headquarters and in Washington, that the mission had been decisive. General Arnold told press correspondents that the cost was high but deemed worth the sacrifice, and announced, "Now we have got Schweinfurt," adding that the "opposition isn't nearly what it was, and we were wearing them down." No one questioned Eighth Air Force estimates, based on carefully selected photos of the Schweinfurt damage. The claim that it would be six months before the Schweinfurt factories could return to full production was impossible to check. The Chief of the Air Staff, Marshal of the Royal Air Force Charles Portal, said, "The Schweinfurt raid may well go down in history as one of the decisive air actions of the war, and it may prove to have saved countless lives by depriving the enemy of a great part of the means of resistance." The raid also seemed to validate the American faith in daylight strategic bombing.

The second Schweinfurt raid did prove to be decisive and a turning point in the daylight bombing campaign, but not for the reasons promulgated by VIII Bomber Command. By mid-October 1943 the daylight bombing campaign had reached a crisis because its cost had risen alarmingly while its successes remained problematical.

Throughout October, 214 bombers – 10 percent of those dispatched – had been lost, and many more damaged. These losses and damages amounted to over half of VIII Bomber Command, and at this rate an entirely new bomber force would be required every three months to maintain the daylight strategic bombing campaign. The four full-strength missions in the second week of October – to Bremen, Marienburg, Münster, and Schweinfurt – had cost the Eighth Air Force 148 heavy bombers, 50 percent of its average daily operational strength. The losses incurred on the Schweinfurt mission – 60 B-17s and crews and major damage to 17 bombers that returned – amounted to more than double the 10-percent-of-force figure that Eighth Air Force considered prohibitive to operations.

Despite some efficiently executed and relatively effective bombing accomplished in the teeth of this concentrated opposition, the month's operations ended in discouragement and a decision to alter for the time being the conduct of the CBO insofar as it involved the American heavy bombers. At that point, Eighth Air Force was in no position to make further penetrations either to Schweinfurt or to any other objectives deep in German territory beyond the range of the P-47 escorts. The USAAF's doctrine of unescorted daylight bombing and self-defending bomber formations was dead. No more deep-penetration raids would be made into Germany until the bombers could be escorted all the way to the target. Eighth Air Force, which had never really managed air superiority over Germany, had for the time being lost even a pretense of it.

Morale at bomber bases was a major problem. The crews had been told time and again that the Luftwaffe fighter force was almost finished, but Fortress crews were currently incurring a casualty rate higher than any other branch of the US forces: during 1943, only about 25 percent of Eighth Air Force bomber crewmen completed their 25-mission tours – the other 75 percent were killed, severely wounded, or captured. It was difficult to persuade the men who survived Schweinfurt that the opposition encountered was the last effort of a beaten force.

Eighth Air Force research stated that "growing enemy fighter power precluded bomber operations to targets deep in Central and Southern Germany until long-range fighters were available to provide full escort." The value of fighter escort had been plainly demonstrated on many occasions – losses of VIII Bomber Command per mission were averaging 1 percent when escorted, 7 percent when not escorted – and it had gradually been elevated to a position of paramount importance in planning future missions. The future of daylight strategic bombing would depend on the presence of fighter escorts with much longer range than the current P-47s, because fighter escort was the only answer to the deadly but relatively unmaneuverable twin-engine rocket-firing German fighters which were peculiarly vulnerable to attacks by other fighters. No one knew this better than Army Air Force commander "Hap" Arnold, and on October 29 he ordered that all P-38 and P-51 production for the next three months was to be withheld from all other theaters and sent to the Eighth, showing the urgency of Eighth Air Force's need for long-range escorts.

Every time a B-17 went down, ten men became casualties, but often a bomber survived an attack and brought back dead or wounded to its base. A casualty is shown being removed after a mission over Germany. (NARA)

The VIII Fighter Command's first P-38s taxiing out after they returned from the Mediterranean, October 15, 1943. It was an orientation mission since they are not carrying external tanks. (NARA)

The German view

The second raid on Schweinfurt damaged only 10 percent of the machines and, as noted, Speer had already reorganized and diversified many of the German industries so thoroughly that any further effort to destroy them would take many concentrated and sustained attacks. The German leadership remained concerned because they knew that much of its war production was concentrated in a few places, all of which were known to Allied intelligence agencies, but American strategic bombing did not seriously affect German military production until mid-1944.

While VIII Bomber Command was making outlandish claims about German losses and claiming that the Luftwaffe was about to collapse, the German air defenses were continuing to increase in strength and effectiveness. The rocket-firing twin-engine fighter was the most effective Luftwaffe weapon, and the B-17's range limitations forced a relatively straight-line routing of the bomber stream and allowed the Luftwaffe controller to see the possible targets and concentrate the defenders in its path to make mass attacks easier.

Although the German fighter force was pressed and suffering a high rate of attrition, it continued to demonstrate and even increase its ability to break up the tight-knit bomber boxes and inflict severe punishment on the unescorted bomber formations. The formula of mass concentration on one bomber formation at a time – usually the one flying the loosest formation – and scattering it further by firing rockets from beyond the effective range of defensive guns, and then repeatedly pressing head-on formation attacks with single-engine fighters, brought success after success.

The attacks on the *Pulks* were dangerous for the RLV fighter pilots and required strong and steady leadership from the fighter leaders, but the Germans had an abundance of that. Again and again the reports of American bomber crews talked of the bravery and skill of the RLV fighter pilots as they pressed the attacks to close range.

Nevertheless, the Germans could only see their weaknesses. They knew that they were inflicting heavy losses on the American bombers, but the American numbers increased because of their production and the Germans could not see an end to the raids. Additionally, they were afraid – justifiably – that the Americans would increase the range of the fighter escorts.

Later in 1943

The weakened Eighth Air Force flew only one more mission in October, on October 20 to Düren, an industrial target in the Ruhr that was close enough to England for full escort. The force was to bomb using the newly acquired British navigation aid, *Oboe*, but the target was covered in clouds and the *Oboe* failed.

November began with a major strategic move by the USAAF, a build-up of the strategic bombing force in Italy so that Germany could be attacked from the south, which would further stretch the German forces. It was also planned to take advantage of the (supposedly) better Italian weather, and allow missions to be mounted on days that the Eighth in England was grounded. Previous raids on Axis industry by B-24s from the south had been successful (except for the low-altitude Ploesti attack where 54 B-24s had been lost) and it was apparent that the German defenses in southern Germany and Austria were still weak. The American Joint Chiefs of Staff sent General Eisenhower a proposed directive, submitted by General Arnold on October 9, calling for the establishment of a new air force (the Fifteenth) in Italy to be used when needed as part of the CBO against strategic targets in Germany. A number of B-24 groups that were scheduled to join the Eighth were sent to the Fifteenth because the B-24s had generally proved inadequate for deep missions into Germany from England.

The Eighth Air Force flew eight escorted raids to close-range German targets in November, beginning on November 3 with a raid on Wilhelmshaven, on which the newly operational P-38 group flew its first mission, an easy section of the withdrawal leg. P-47s provided ingress escort to the short-range target, and the German fighters were hampered severely by bad weather and lost 16 of their number, while only nine B-17s were shot down. US air activity over the Reich remained at a low level through December, with only seven missions to Germany, and all but one of the raids were well within the escort fighters' range.

Strategic consequences

The operational crisis of October within the Eighth Air Force coincided with a crisis in planning for the entire air war in Europe. The crisis centered upon the defeat of the Luftwaffe day fighter force, the *sine qua non* for the success of Operation *Overlord*, the invasion of France. *Overlord* was scheduled for May 1944, but before the invasion could safely be attempted the Allied strategic air forces would have to gain air superiority over western Europe, and that meant defeating the fighter force.

In October the CBO had come to the end of its second planned phase, and it was a matter of the utmost concern to Allied planners to determine if the American daylight bombing force had accomplished its task of defeating the Luftwaffe day fighter force. There were still certain doubts and questions about the efficacy of these daylight operations, and while VIII Bomber Command had demonstrated that no parts of the Reich could be considered immune from daylight attack, the Luftwaffe day fighter force could still set a high, possibly even a prohibitive, cost on these raids, and Eighth Air Force could not claim it had air superiority.

When the Combined Chiefs of Staff met for the Sextant Conference in early December they were told that the Luftwaffe was rapidly expanding its fighter strength in Germany, and USAAF commander General Arnold dismayed the CCS when he was forced to announce that the American buildup in England had fallen well behind the rate of reinforcement that planners had stated was necessary to achieve *Pointblank*'s objectives. Privately, Arnold also strongly expressed his displeasure with Eaker, complaining that while other theaters were using 60–70 percent of their aircraft, Eighth was using only 50 percent, and in their December 3 report the CCS stated that "General Eaker should be told to expand his operations to the extent possible with the aircraft and crews available."

The solution

The key to air superiority over Germany was shooting down RLV fighters in the air, not, at this point, bombing the factories, but this meant not paying attention to the exaggerated claims of the B-17 gunners, which had been accepted for virtually the entire campaign.

Even before Arnold's order of October 29, the first step was already underway in October 1943 when truly long-range P-38 fighters began to return to England from the Mediterranean

The P-38 had the range but not the performance to escort the bombers and often suffered heavily at the hands of RLV single-engine fighters. (NARA)

theater after a year's absence. The Lightnings carried twin 150-gallon drop tanks and had a useful combat radius of about 500 miles, a considerable improvement over the P-47s which, even with the new 108-gallon belly tanks that had arrived in August and September 1943, had a combat radius of just 300 miles. One understrength group of P-38s was already in England and became operational on October 15, 1943, while another group of P-38s began operations in December 1943.

But despite its long range, the P-38 had encountered difficulty in coping with German fighters in North Africa, and on November 19 it showed it had the same problem over Europe when, in extended dogfights with RLV single-seat fighters, nine P-38s were shot down.

The real answer was the long-range P-51B Mustang, which would prove to be in most respects the best fighter of the war, but it did not become available for combat until December 1943. Moreover, because the first model, the P-51A, had been a low-altitude fighter, General Eaker sent the first P-51B units to join the tactical Ninth Air Force when it reached England to "simplify maintenance and repair," while the Eighth took the new P-47 units. This did not sit well with Arnold, who had been pushing Eaker to improve fighter escorts to cut bomber losses and who understood what the role of the P-51Bs should be. The immediate reaction of the short-fuzed Arnold when he learned of this agreement is unrecorded, but he quickly forced Eaker to rescind it.

The savior arrives. A P-51B visiting an Eighth Air Force bomber base in December 1943. It has a white cowling and white stripes on the wings and tail as identity markings to distinguish it from a Bf 109. The long-range P-51 was quickly to gain air superiority over Europe and in many ways made D-Day possible. (NARA)

ANALYSIS AND CONCLUSIONS

The American campaign objective for the 1943 daylight bombing missions deep into Germany was to cripple the Luftwaffe fighter force in order to provide the air superiority vital for the invasion of France, Operation *Overlord*, to be successful. Eighth Air Force was unable to achieve this campaign objective because the Germans were able to fulfill their own objective of destroying so many Eighth Air Force bombers that the Americans stopped their bombing campaign in mid-October 1943.

The Germans were able to accomplish this success because Galland and Milch convinced Göring to move much of the Luftwaffe's day fighter force from the eastern and southern periphery to Germany, where prior to 1943 there had hardly been any day fighters. By mid-1943 the air defense of Germany proper was reinforced by day fighter forces from units in Russia and the Mediterranean, and many other improvements were under way. New tactics were developed, command and control improved, the production of both fighter pilots and planes was increased, and new anti-bomber weapons were introduced, especially the combination most feared by VIII Bomber Command, the Wfr. Gr. 21 rockets on the twin-engine Bf 110s and Me 410s.

The Luftwaffe also had an advantage because the American bombing campaign developed slowly, and the Germans were able to match the increasing number of American bombers by importing fighter units. The slow pace of the American campaign also allowed the Luftwaffe to continually upgrade its command and control procedures and develop its system of auxiliary airfields so that it could mobilize its fighters along the bombers' route and the pilots could fly two missions against the raids. The slow increase also gave the Luftwaffe time to develop tactics for the combination of rocket-firing fighters attacking in concert with the single-seat fighters, tactics which led to the disastrous American losses in October 1943.

On the American side, the main reason for their failure was a doctrinal one. The basic maxim was that American heavy bombers could defend themselves, so the Army Air

A P-51B having its external fuel tank seated. Given the bomb sortie markings under the cockpit, this may have been very early in 1944 when the P-51s were briefly attached to Ninth Air Force as attack aircraft rather than as bomber escorts. General Arnold quickly intervened and had the P-51s assigned to VIII Fighter Command for bomber escort duties. (NARA)

Force failed to develop a long-range escort fighter that could accompany the bombers. In the skies over Germany the idea of the "self-defending bomber" proved to be fatally flawed. The other part of the doctrine focused on very accurate bombing of high-value targets, but here European weather played a major role because the American bombers were unable to hit many of their targets owing to cloud cover. But even with the problems hitting the targets, the main reason that the daylight bombing campaign into Germany was terminated in mid-October 1943 was the heavy losses inflicted by the German day fighters.

However, this American failure was disguised for most of 1943 because of the exaggerated claims of the bombers' gunners. As VIII Bomber Command continued its unescorted raids into Germany through October 1943 and continued to suffer brutal losses, the leadership was telling both Washington and the crews that they were winning the battle because of the numbers of German fighters they were shooting down. This exaggeration was probably a blessing in disguise, since had the real figures been known to Arnold and VIII Bomber Command the campaign might have been terminated. Almost certainly, if the bomber crews had known how few German fighters they were destroying, morale would have collapsed.

Much more accurate figures of the true German losses were available, but the Eighth Air Force leadership ignored these numbers. This failure to understand that they were not shooting down as many Germans as they thought kept Eighth Air Force from a real sense of urgency in procuring really useful external fuel tanks for the P-47 and even calling for the return of the long-range P-38s from Africa. A good deal of the blame for this must go to the commander of Eighth Air Force, General Ira Eaker, who, instead of making a real effort to develop an effective escort fighter force by prioritizing reliable external fuel tanks, supported short-term fixes like the YB-40.

But despite their success, many in the Luftwaffe leadership knew how fragile their victory in late 1943 was. Their most effective weapon, the heavily armed twin-engine *Zerstörer*, was helpless against single-engine fighters, and even the American P-47s were slowly increasing their range as more and better external tanks were beginning to be delivered. Galland was alarmed and warned Göring, but Göring did not believe him, and even if he had there was little the Germans could do.

In fact, even in October the battle was shifting. The first long-range, twin-engine P-38s had returned from Africa and were almost ready to fly combat missions from England, but VIII Bomber Command had given up on the deep bombing raids before they could be used. The P-38 would have been very effective against the *Zerstörer*, but the Luftwaffe single-seat fighters had proven to be superior in North Africa and in the first combats with the P-38s in Europe the German single-seaters continued their domination.

The real solution to the escort issue had actually been flying in the United Kingdom in one form since January 1942: the RAF Mustang Mark 1a, known in the United States as the P-51A. But while it had extraordinary range and the airframe was excellent, the Allison V-12 engine was only good at low altitude. The RAF re-engined one with the Rolls-Royce Merlin which gave it the high-altitude performance needed, and after some bureaucratic delays the USAAF adopted the idea; by December 1943, the first Merlin-powered P-51Bs were arriving in England. Unfortunately, Eaker first directed that they be sent to Ninth Air Force for use as ground attack aircraft; however, Arnold intervened and all the P-51Bs were sent to VIII Fighter Command. By January 1944, P-51Bs were beginning to dominate the skies over Germany and produced the great aerial victories of 1944 that destroyed, for practical purposes, any chance the Luftwaffe had of threatening D-Day.

INDEX